TRICKY TRIDOKU

JAPHETH J. LIGHT

PUZZLE
WRIGHT
PRESS

New York

**PUZZLE
WRIGHT
PRESS**

New York

An Imprint of Sterling Publishing
387 Park Avenue South
New York, NY 10016

© 2012 by Japheth J. Light

ISBN 978-1-4027-8143-8

Distributed in Canada by Sterling Publishing
C/o Canadian Manda Group, 165 Dufferin Street
Toronto, Ontario, Canada M6K 3H6
Distributed in the United Kingdom by GMC Distribution Services
Castle Place, 166 High Street, Lewes, East Sussex, England BN7 1XU
Distributed in Australia by Capricorn Link (Australia) Pty. Ltd.
P.O. Box 704, Windsor, NSW 2756, Australia

For information about custom editions, special sales, and premium and corporate purchases,
please contact Sterling Special Sales at 800-805-5489 or specialsales@sterlingpublishing.com.

Printed in China

2 4 6 8 10 9 7 5 3 1

CONTENTS

To my wife, Monica

INTRODUCTION

I'm excited to present a second book of puzzles for Tridoku fans. The book is similar to the first Tridoku book, but although the puzzles still start out easy, the toughest ones are trickier this time around.

Tridoku is very similar to sudoku, and uses some of the same logic to solve, but the different rules mean that new strategies are also required. Like sudoku, it is simple to understand, but challenging in the logic that the puzzles require.

The rules of sudoku state that:
- The numbers 1–9 must be placed in each of the nine large boxes.
- The numbers 1–9 must be placed in each row.
- The numbers 1–9 must be placed in each column.

The rules of Tridoku are similar:
- The numbers 1–9 must be placed in each of the nine large triangles.
- The numbers 1–9 must be placed in the three legs of the inner shaded triangle.
- The numbers 1–9 must be placed in the three legs of the outer shaded triangle.

Adding to the uniqueness of Tridoku is a fourth rule:
- No two neighboring cells may contain the same number. (Cells that touch along an edge or at a single point are considered neighbors.)

For a more in-depth explanation of the rules and some techniques used to solve the puzzles, please turn to page 7. Or if you're feeling bold, you can jump right into the puzzles, which start on page 14!

—Japheth J. Light

HOW TO SOLVE TRIDOKU

Rule #1: The Large Triangle Rule

The numbers 1–9 must be placed in each of the nine large triangles in the puzzle.

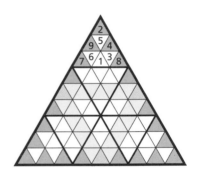

Rule #2: The Inner Triangle Rule

The numbers 1–9 must be placed in each of the three legs of the inner shaded triangle.

Notice that the numbers in the corners of the inner triangle will each count for two legs of the inner triangle. So the 3 in the left corner counts as the 3 for both the top shaded leg and the left shaded leg of the inner triangle.

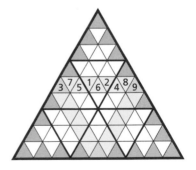

Rule #3: The Outer Triangle Rule

The numbers 1–9 must be placed in each of the three legs of the outer shaded triangle.

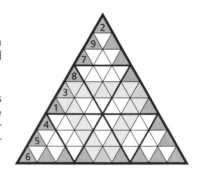

As in Rule #2, the numbers at the corners each lie in two legs of the outer triangle (i.e., the 2 at the top counts as the 2 for both the left and right leg of the outer triangle).

Rule #4: The Hexagon Rule

No two neighboring cells may contain the same numbers.

This rule goes for any two cells that touch—including both cells that share an edge and cells that meet at a single point.

In other words, no numbers can be repeated within any small hexagon in the entire puzzle.

Tips and Strategies

Tridoku is a logic puzzle in which you use the rules defined above—and the process of elimination—to fill in the puzzle. Since Tridoku is a fairly new puzzle, many advanced techniques are still being explored. In this section you will find some basic steps to get you started.

• Power Cells

Perhaps the easiest (and most productive) way to start a puzzle is with Power Cells. These are cells that are centered along an outer edge of a large triangle.

There are 18 Power Cells in each puzzle, but not all of them will contain givens at the start of the puzzle.

A Power Cell is particularly helpful because it uses the Hexagon Rule to reduce the number of cells within a triangle that can contain a given number.

In the example at right, we see that the 2 circled in red is a Power Cell that prevents a 2 from occupying any of the lower 5 cells of the top triangle.

As a result of the Outer Triangle Rule, the 2 circled in blue in the lower left triangle prevents the top cell from being a 2.

The only cell remaining in the top large triangle is the one highlighted in green. This cell must contain a 2.

Power Cells located on the inverted inner triangle can be even more helpful. They effectively "cross out" 6 cells within the target triangle rather than 5. In the example at right, the 2 circled in red prevents a 2 from appearing in all but one of the available cells in the triangle below it; the cell highlighted in green must therefore contain a 2.

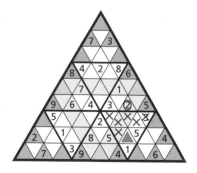

Power Cells can be a great way to start a puzzle, but be warned: the more difficult puzzles in the book contain few (if any) Power Cells at the start of the puzzle.

• Filling In the Inner Triangle

After making as much progress as possible filling in the large triangles, it can be helpful to look for numbers that go in the inner triangle.

Because of the Inner Triangle Rule, the numbers 1–9 must lie in each leg of the inner triangle. This tells us that a 4 must lie somewhere on the left leg of that triangle.

The 4 circled in red prohibits another 4 from appearing in any of the cells marked with a red X. Similarly, the 4 circled in blue prevents a 4 from occupying the cells marked with a blue X.

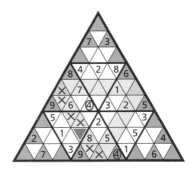

For the left leg of the inner triangle, this leaves only the cell highlighted in green. This cell must be the 4.

• Filling In the Outer Triangle

The Outer Triangle Rule states that each leg of the outer shaded triangle must contain the numbers 1–9. Therefore, the lower leg of the outer triangle must contain a 1.

In the grid at right, the 1 circled in red keeps a 1 from appearing in the middle cells. Similarly, the 1 circled in blue blocks the cells on the right. Finally, the 1 circled in purple prevents a 1 from occupying the far left cell.

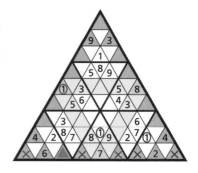

This leaves only the cell highlighted in green, which must be a 1.

• Making Notations

One strategy that many puzzlers find helpful (especially with more difficult puzzles) is to pencil in some notes to help narrow down possibilities later in the puzzle. Be careful, though—too many markings can lead to a cluttered puzzle or increase the chances of making a mistake.

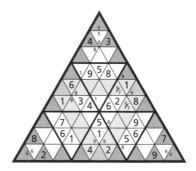

• Finishing the Puzzle

As shown in the discussion of Power Cells, the Hexagon Rule can be a powerful tool when solving a puzzle. In fact, the final cells of a puzzle will generally be determined by the Hexagon Rule. When only a few empty cells remain, examine the surrounding cells, and use the Hexagon Rule to complete the puzzle.

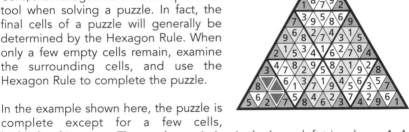

In the example shown here, the puzzle is complete except for a few cells, highlighted in green. The numbers missing in the lower left triangle are 1, 4, and 9. The first three rules offer no clues for filling in these cells.

The placement of these numbers is dictated by the immediate neighbors of those cells. A 1 cannot appear in the lower two triangles, and a 4 cannot appear in either of the upper two. This leaves a 1 on the top, a 4 on the bottom, and the 9 in the middle.

There are 180 puzzles in this book of increasing difficulty—45 each of easy, medium, hard, and "monster" Tridoku. The difficulty levels are indicated on each page with small triangles. (Easy puzzles get one triangle, up to four for "monster.") Enjoy!

—Japheth J. Light

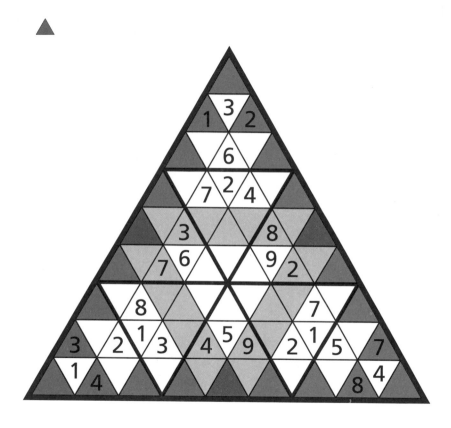

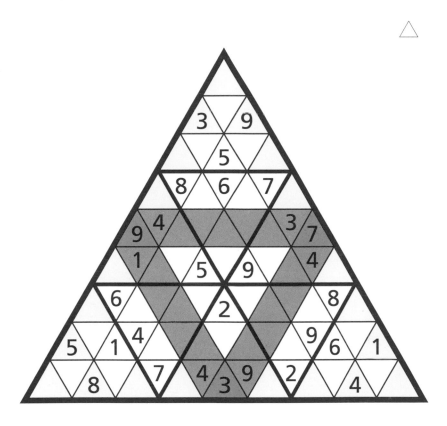

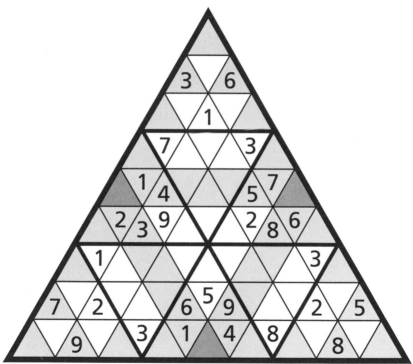

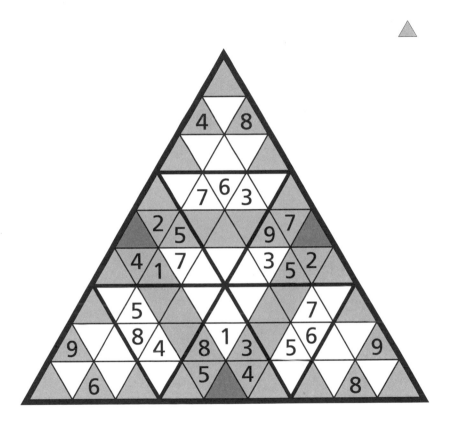

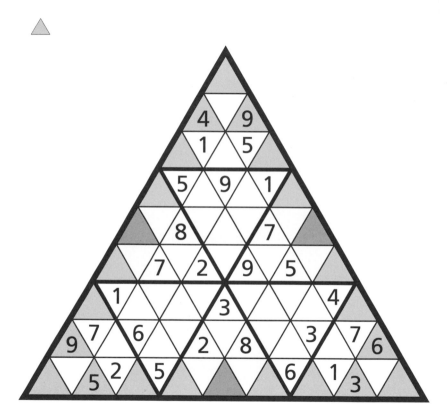

18

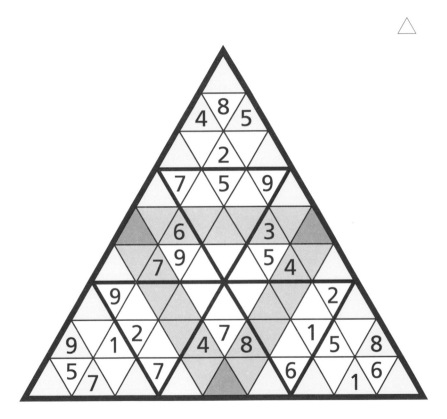

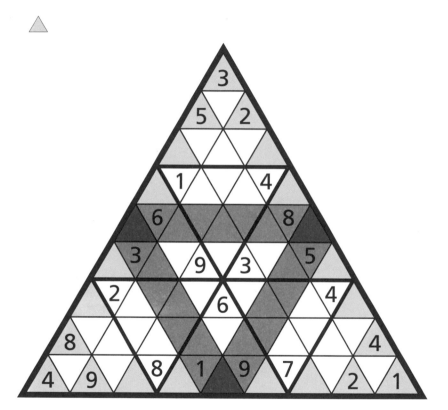

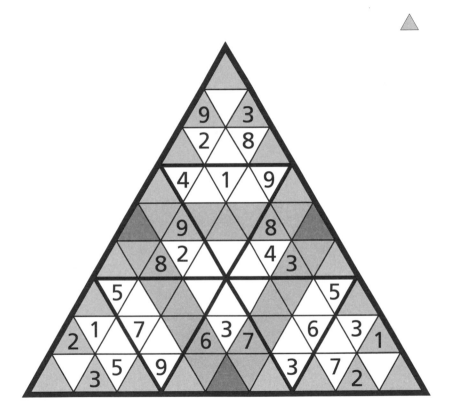

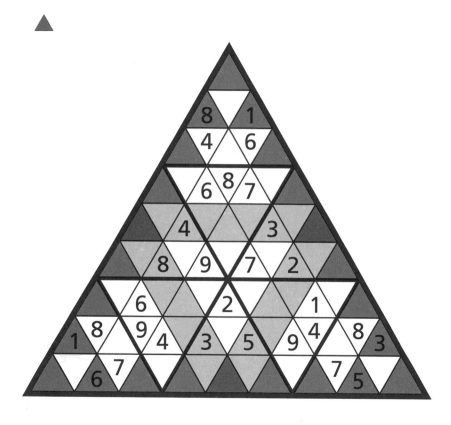

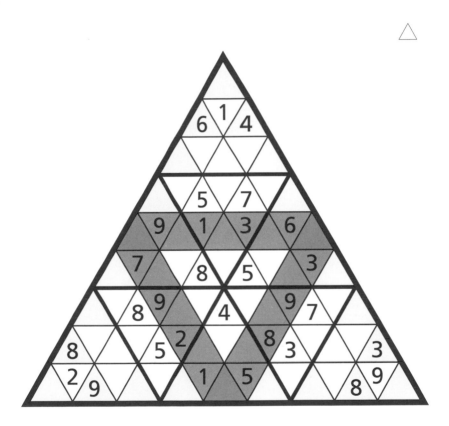

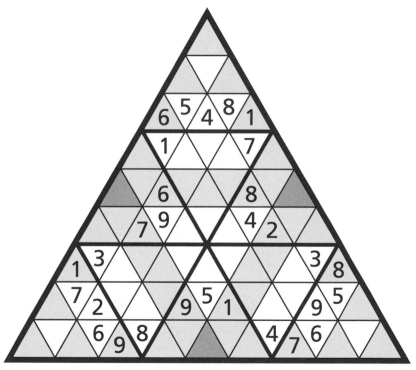

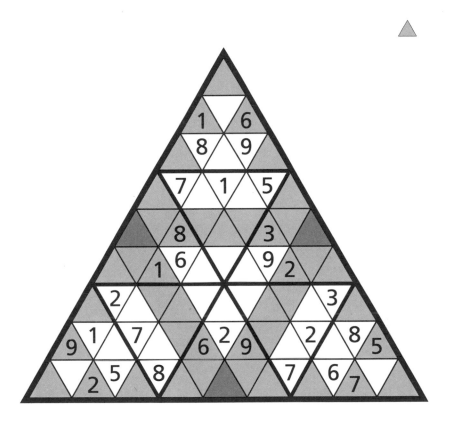

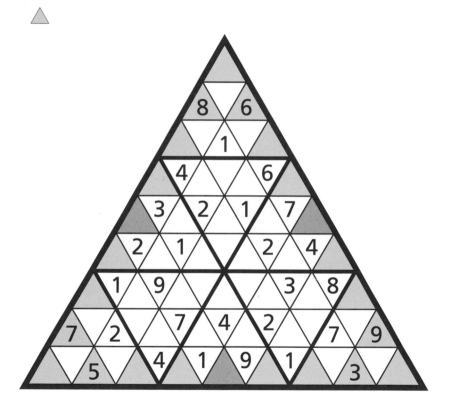

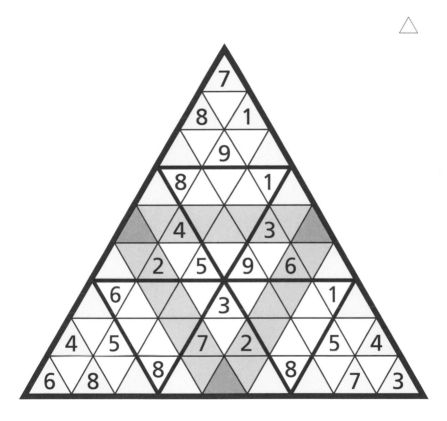

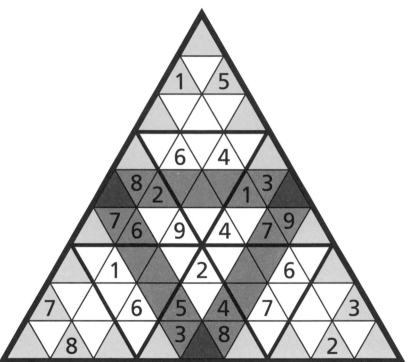

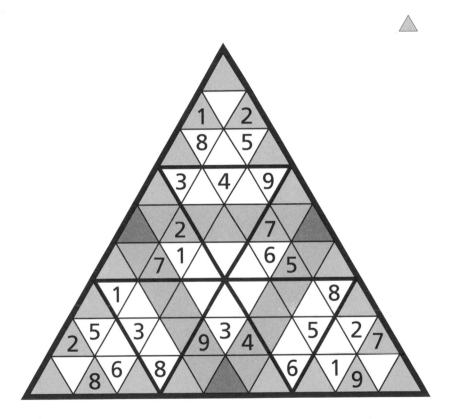

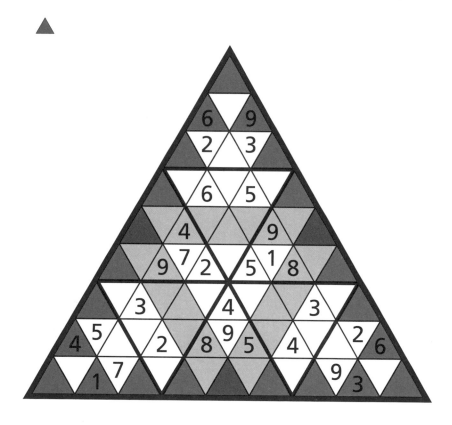

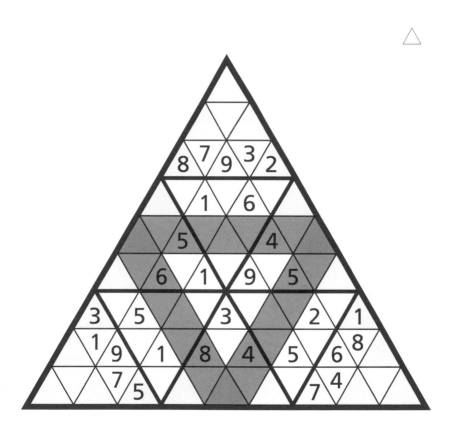

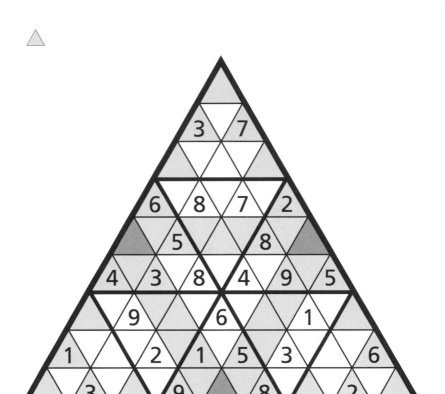

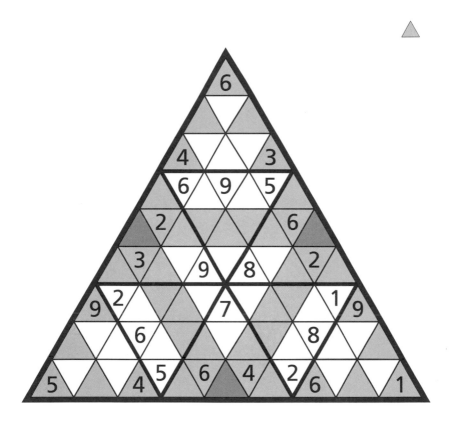

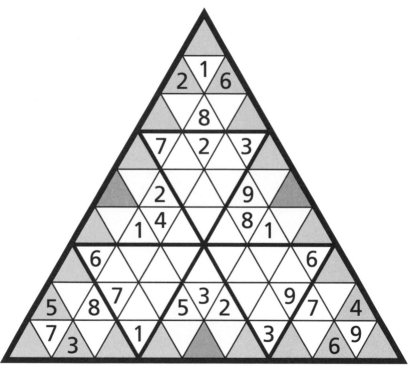

34

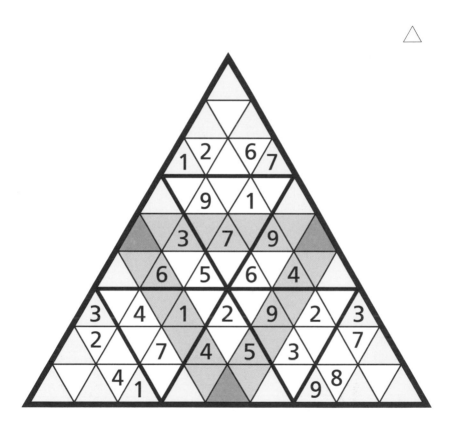

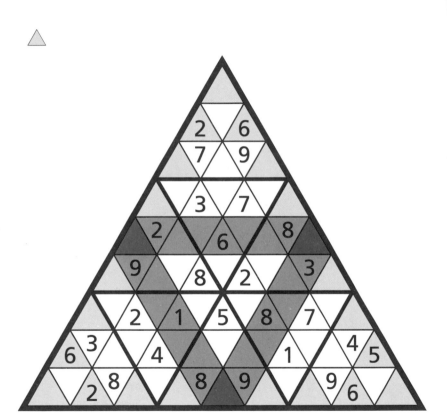

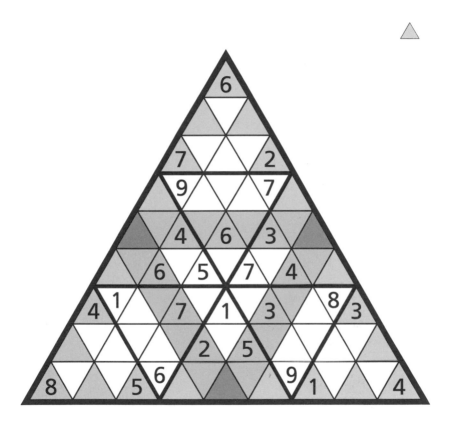

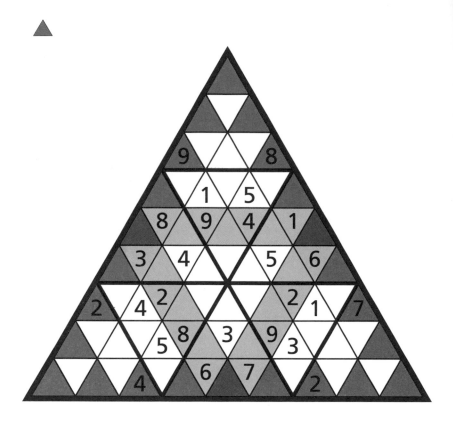

38

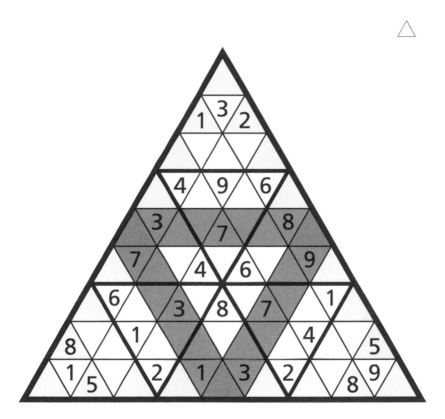

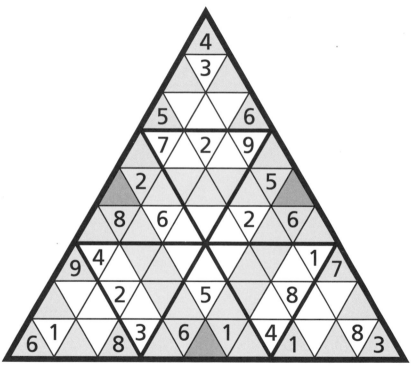

40

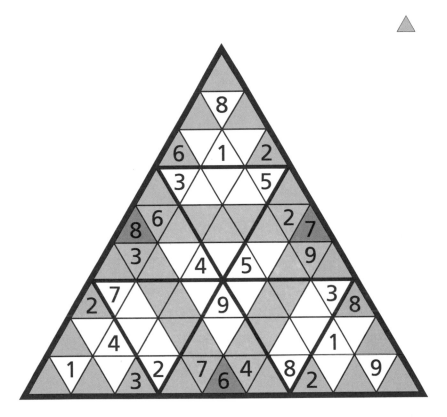

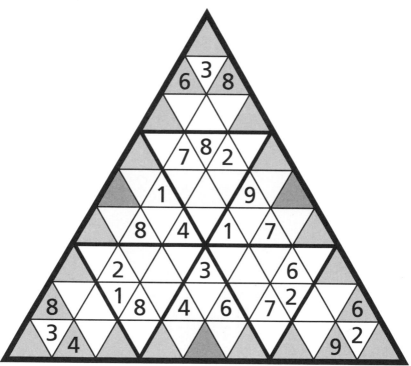

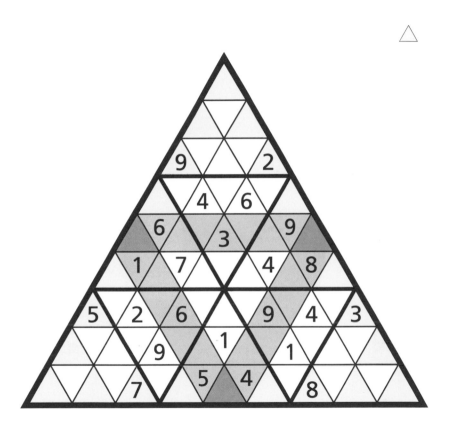

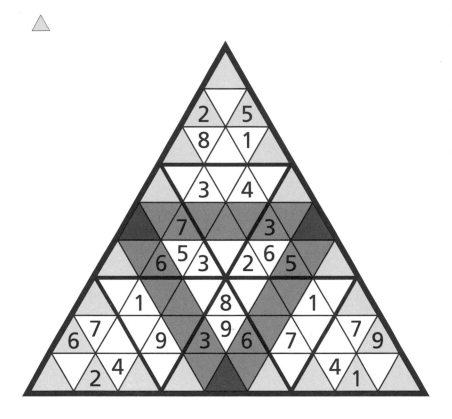

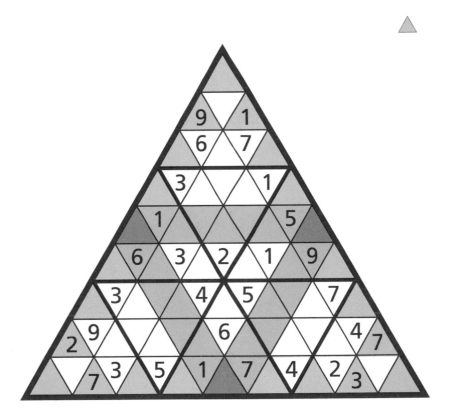

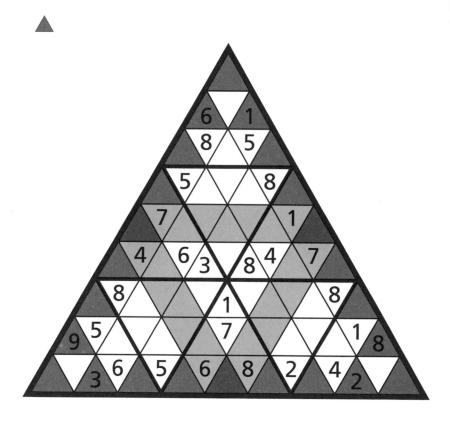

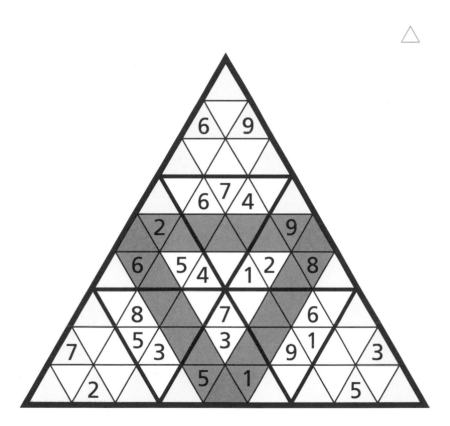

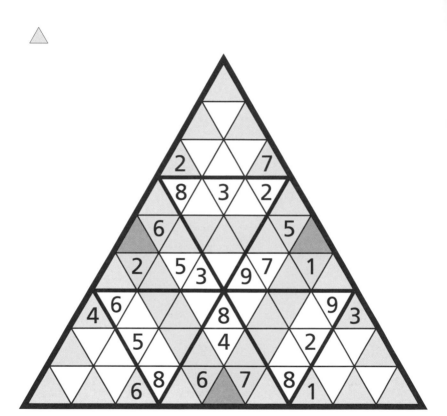

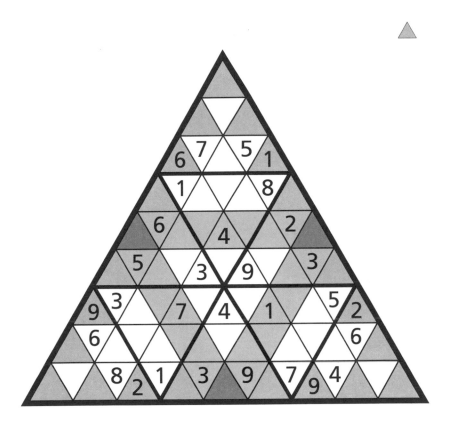

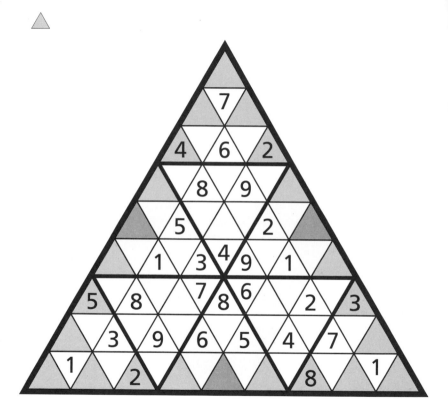

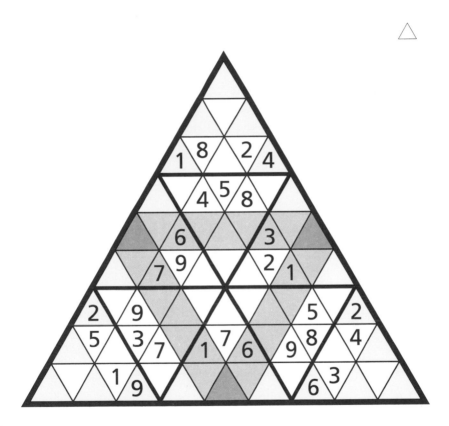

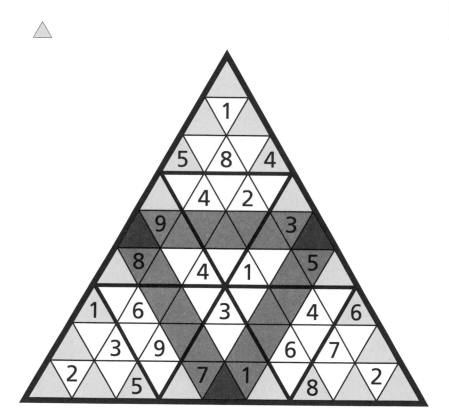

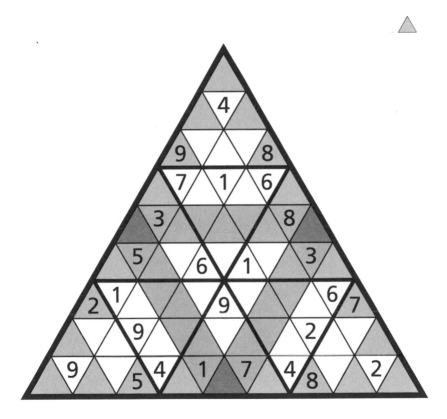

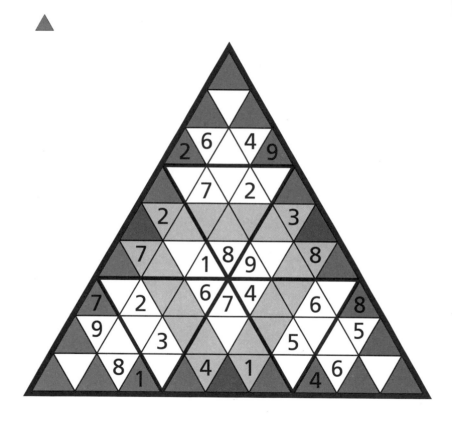

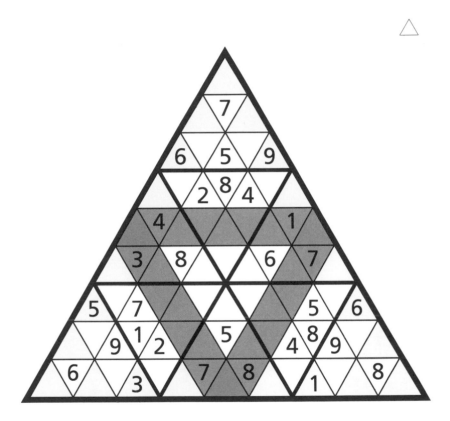

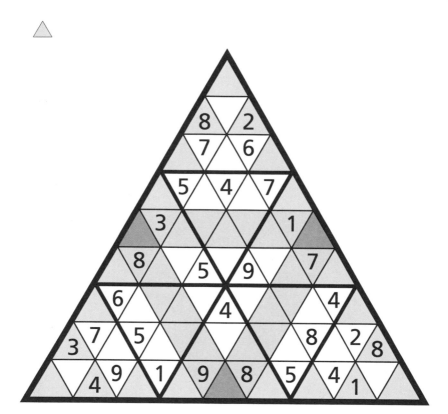

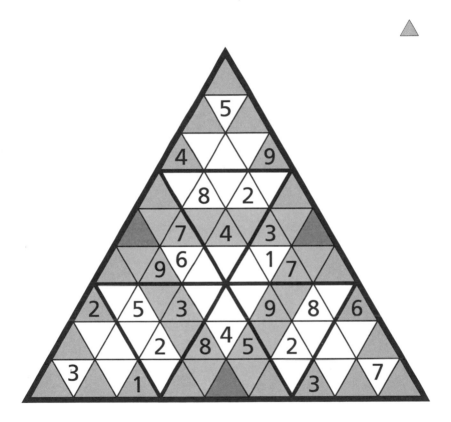

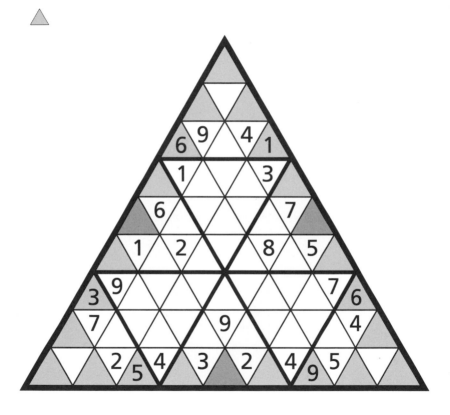

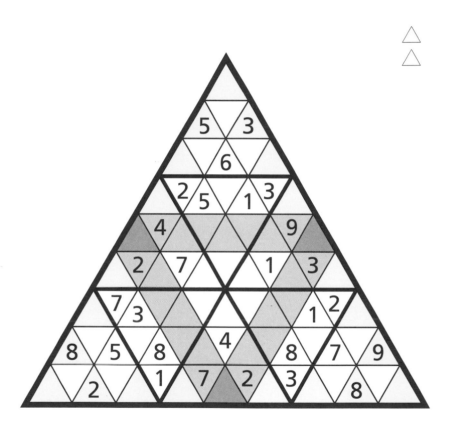

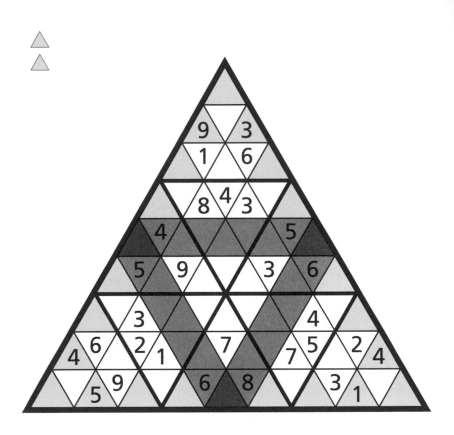

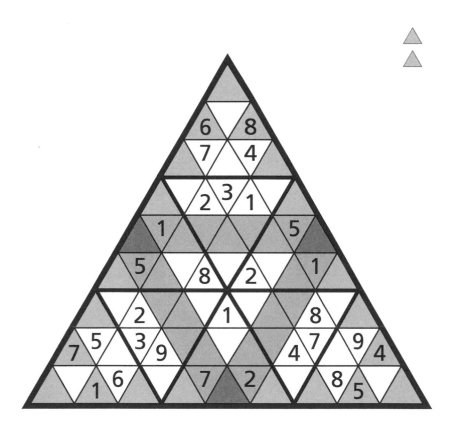

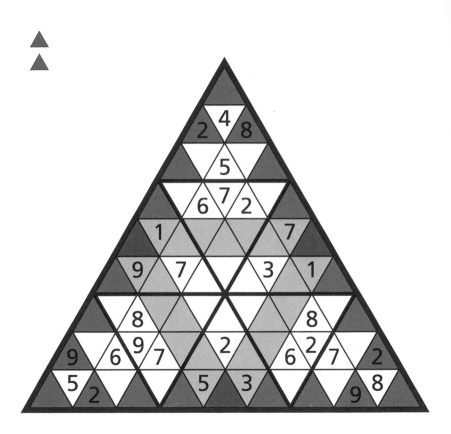

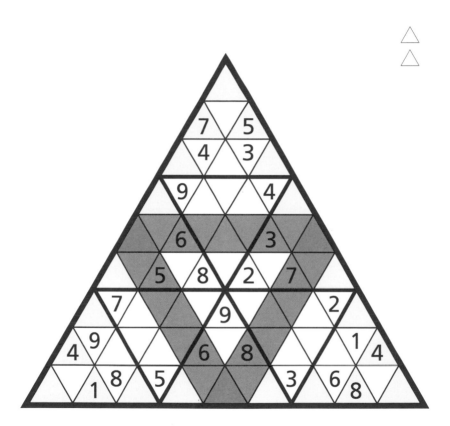

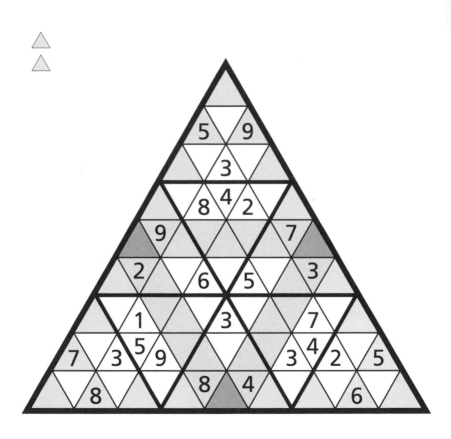

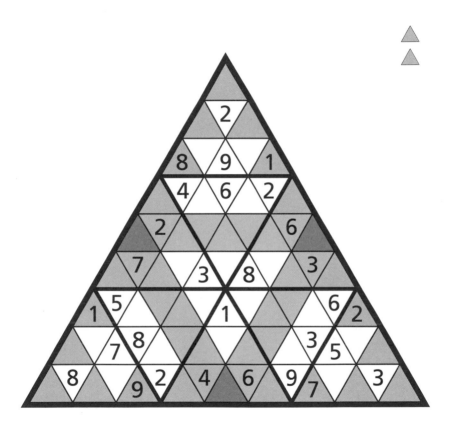

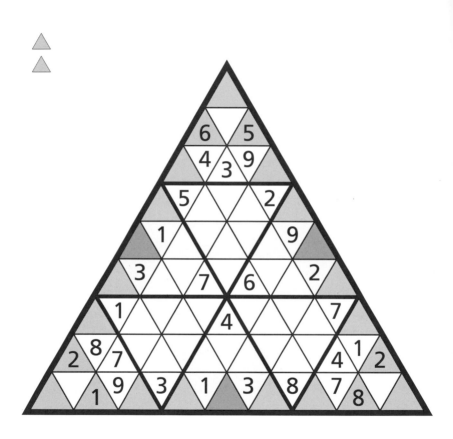

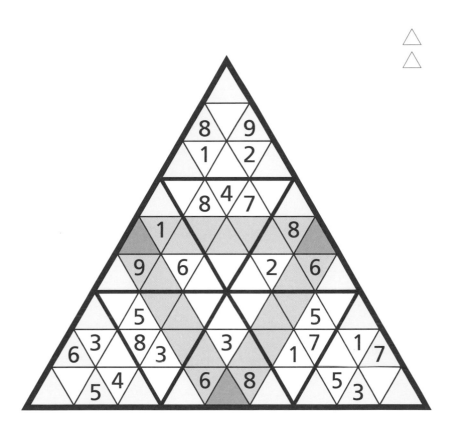

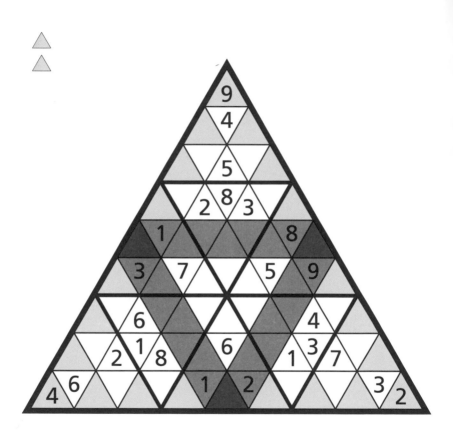

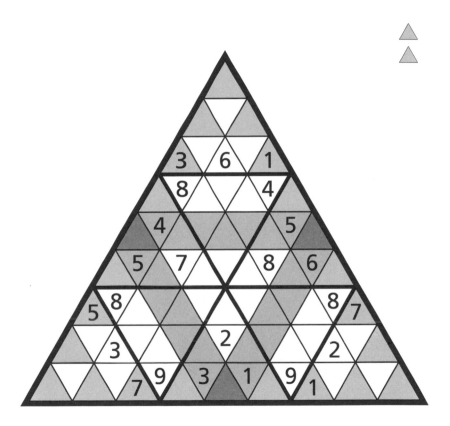

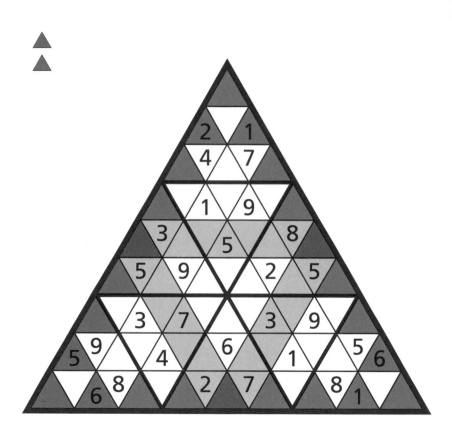

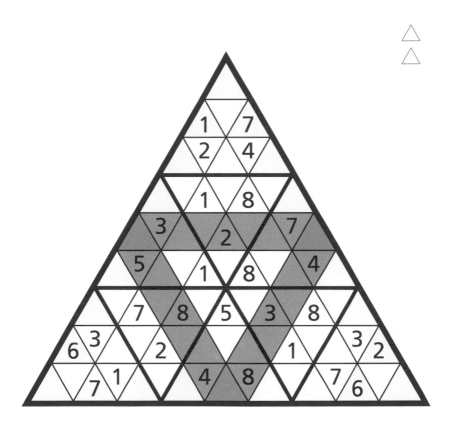

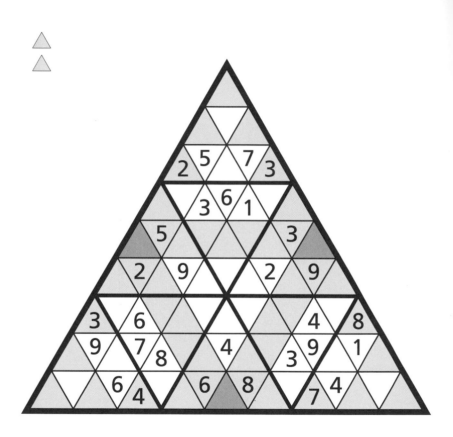

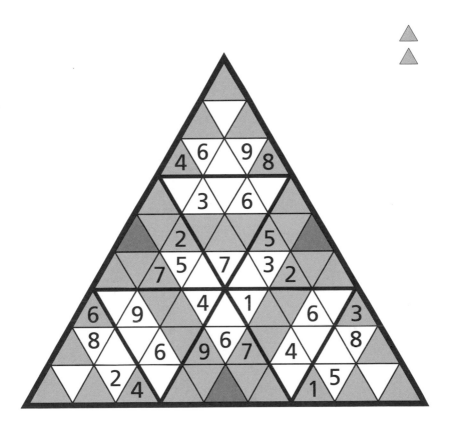

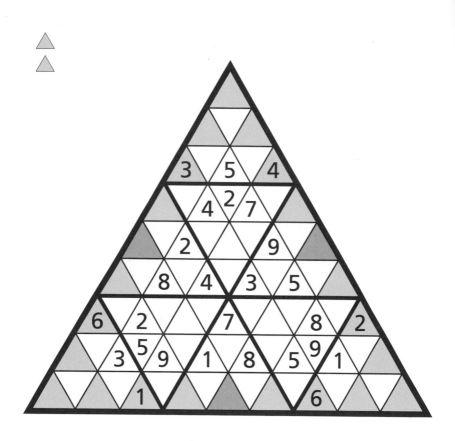

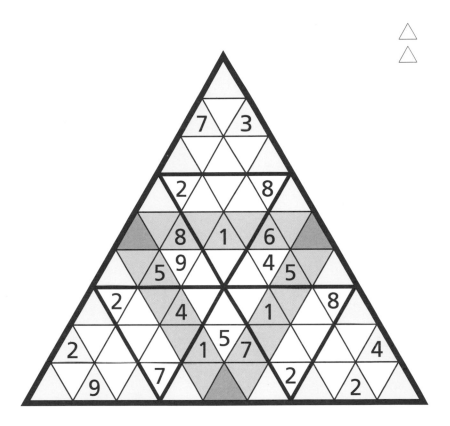

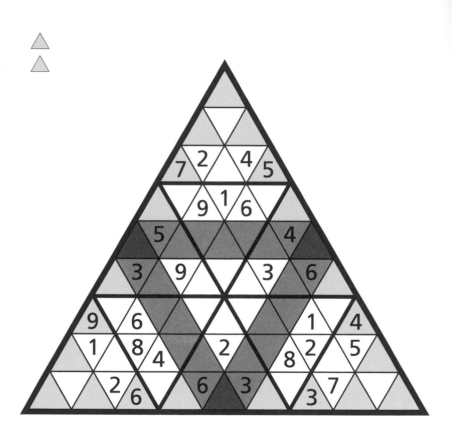

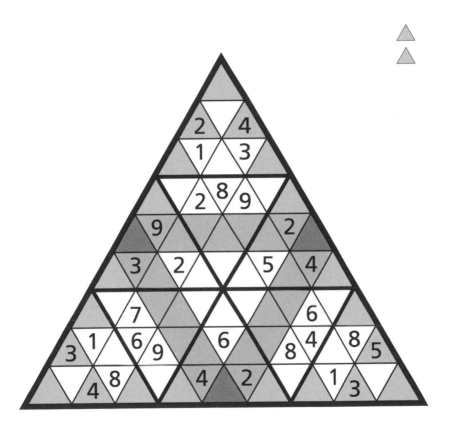

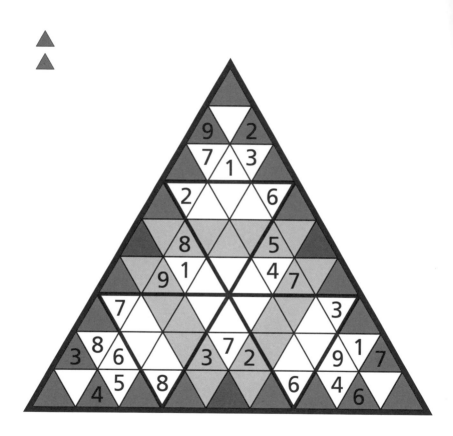

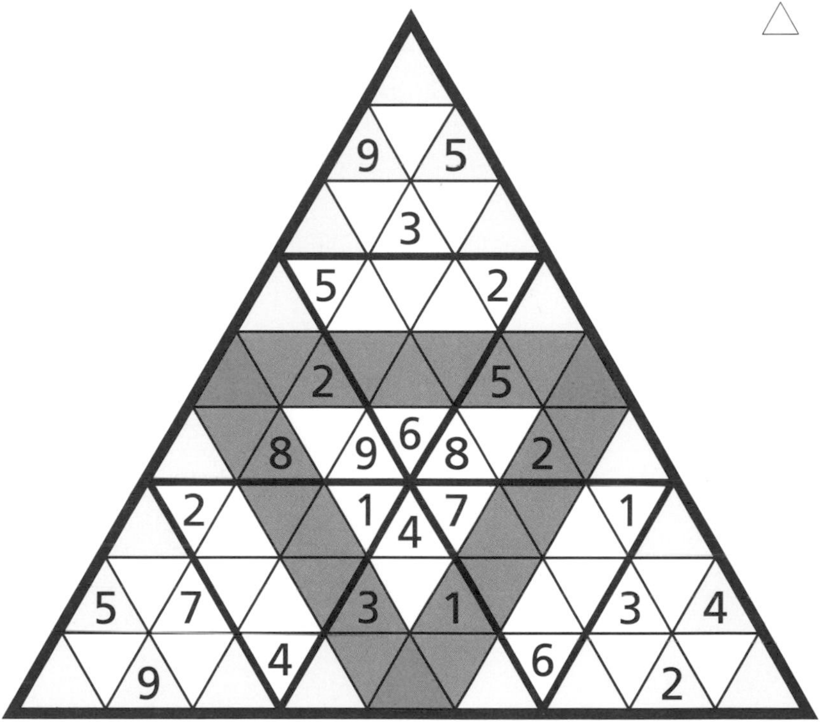
9
5
3
5
2
2
5
8
9
6
8
2
2
1
4
7
1
5
7
3
1
3
4
4
6
9
2

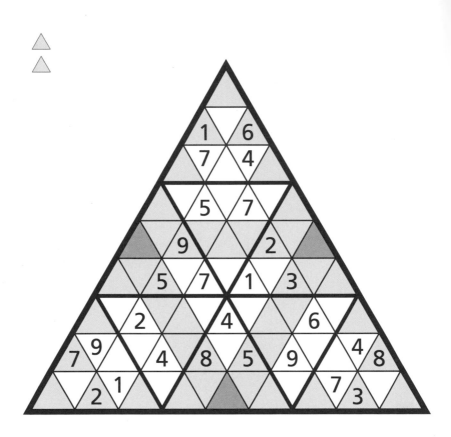

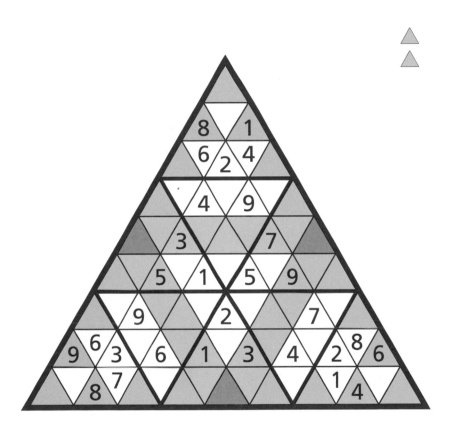

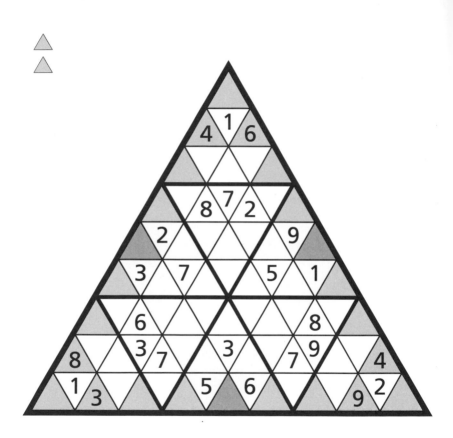

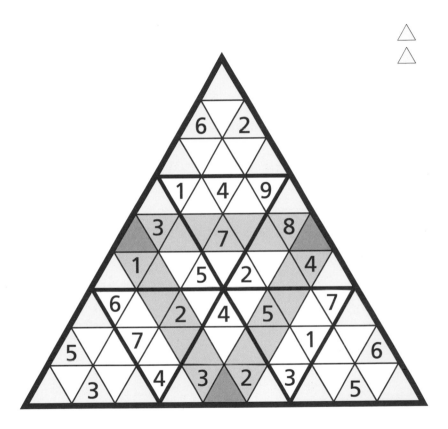

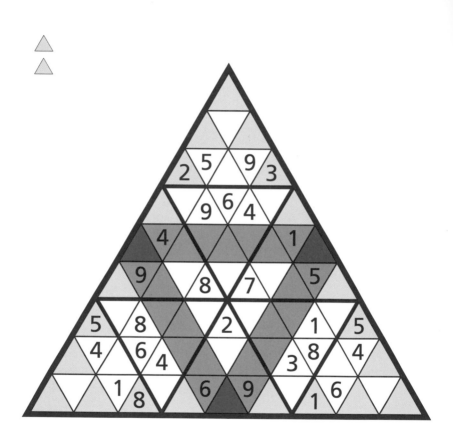

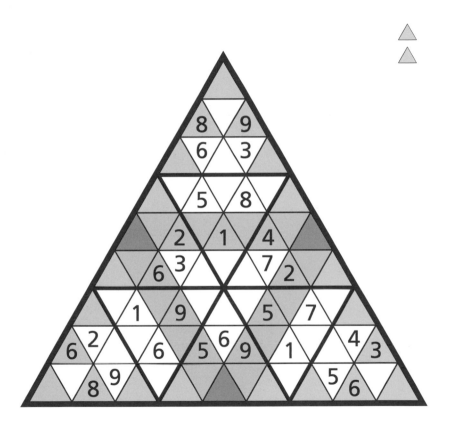

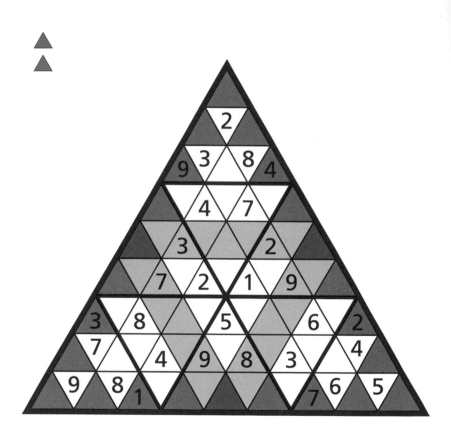

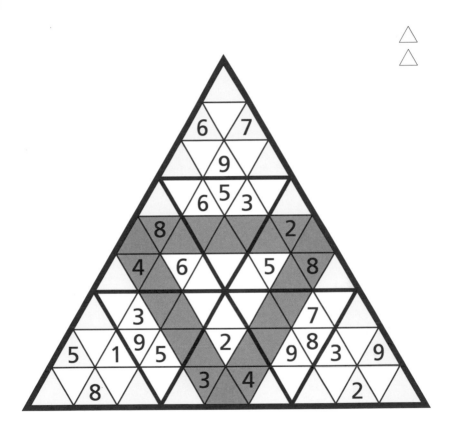

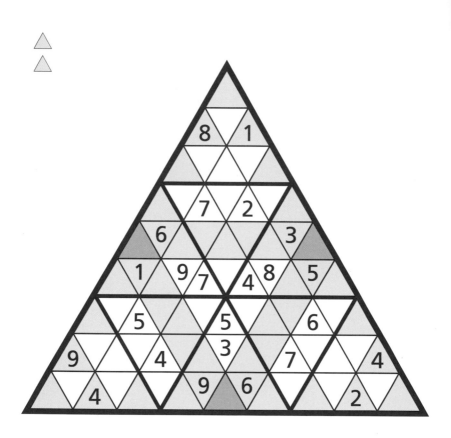

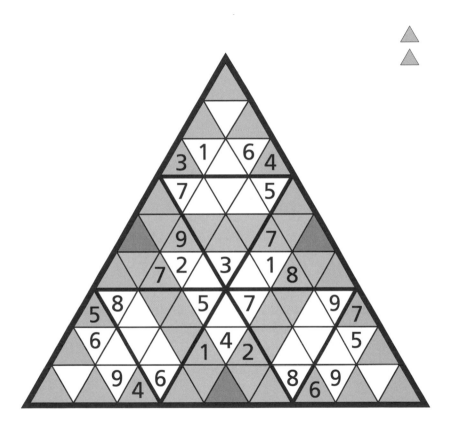

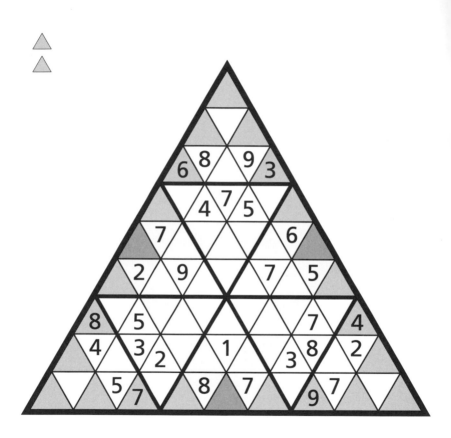

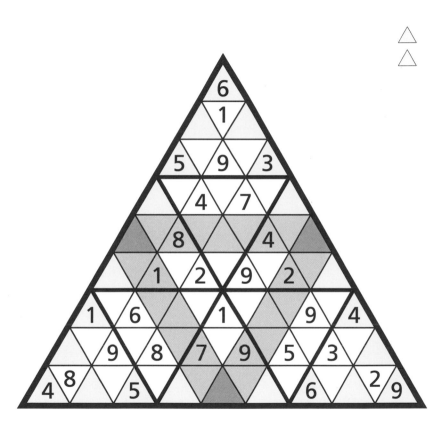

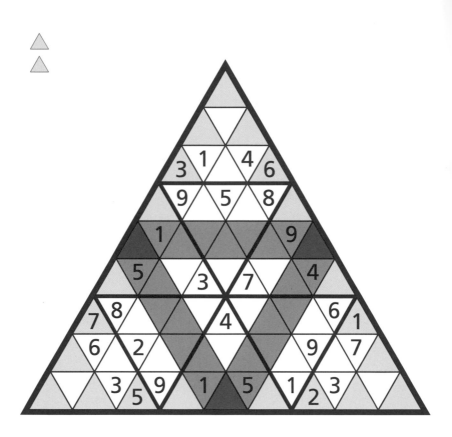

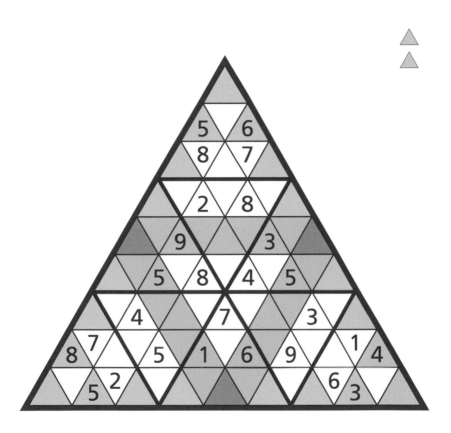

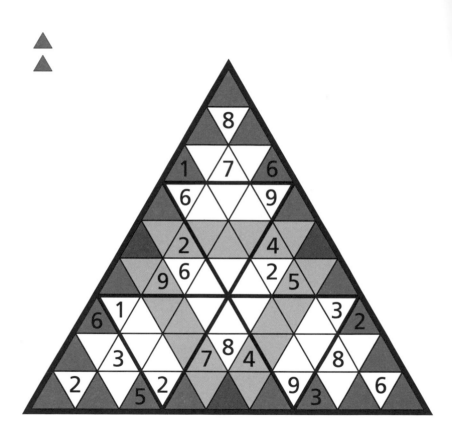

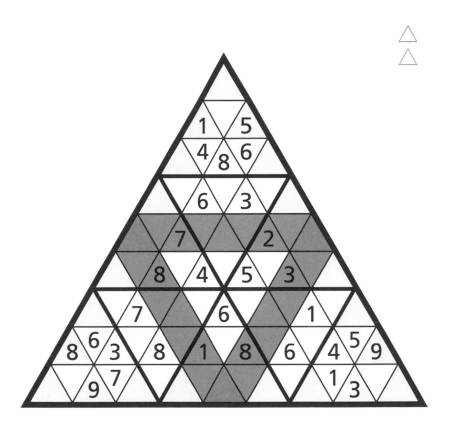

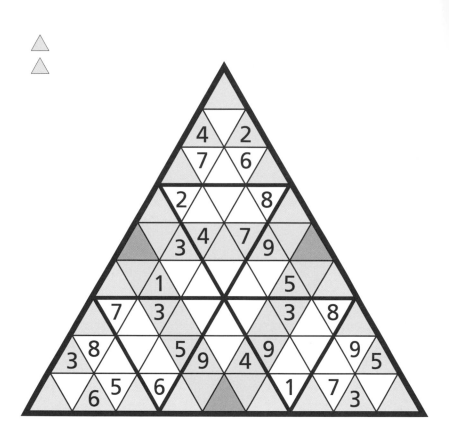

96

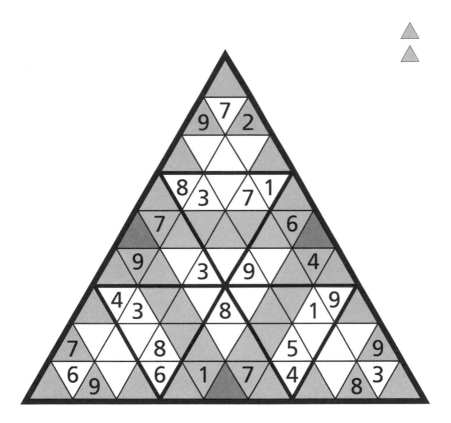

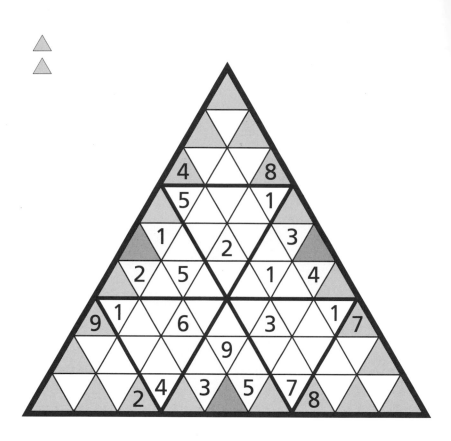

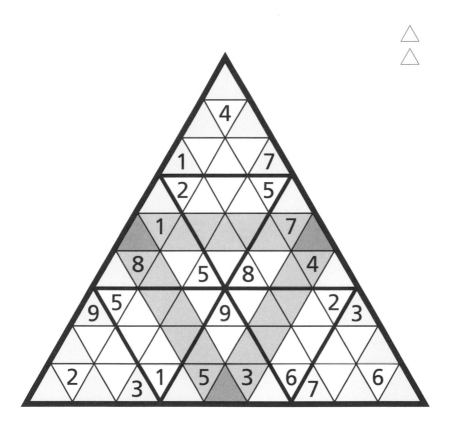

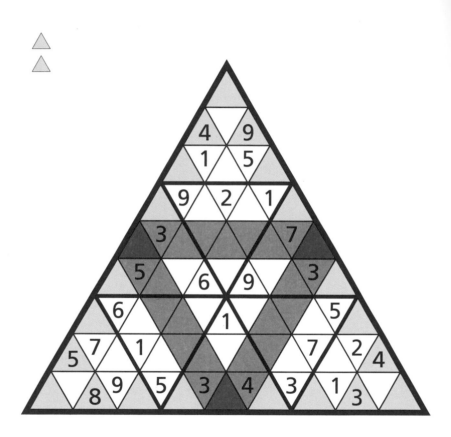

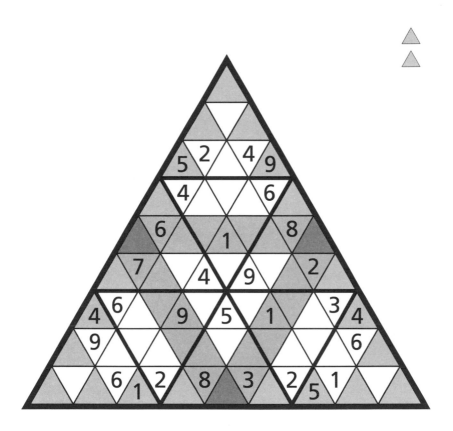

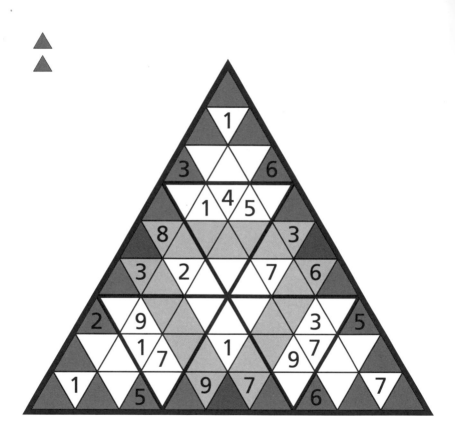

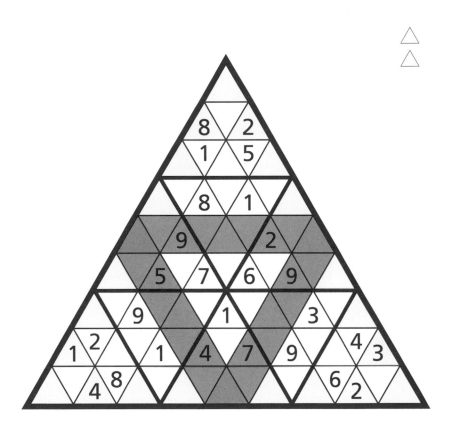

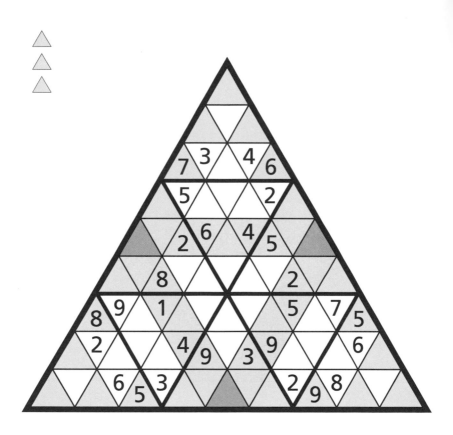

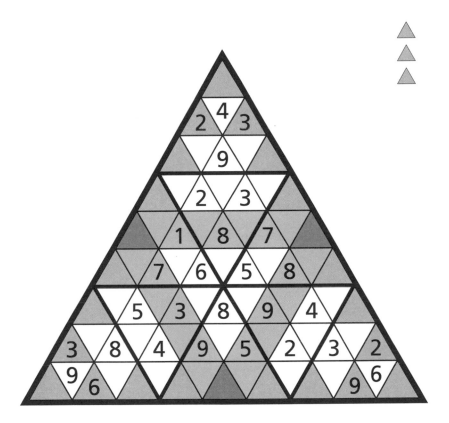

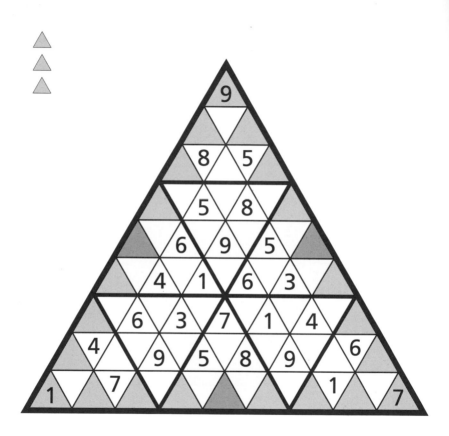

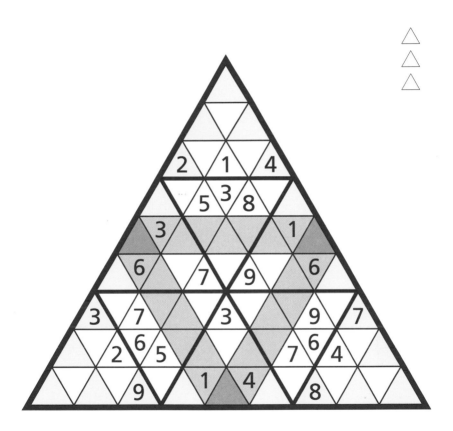

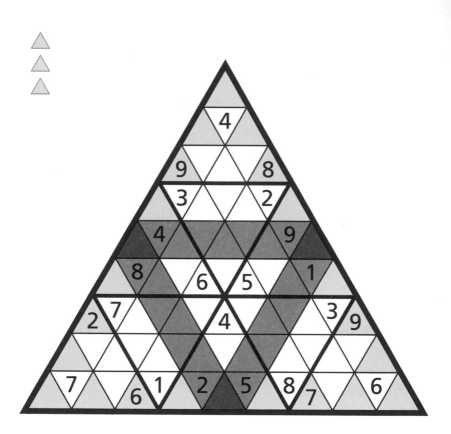

108

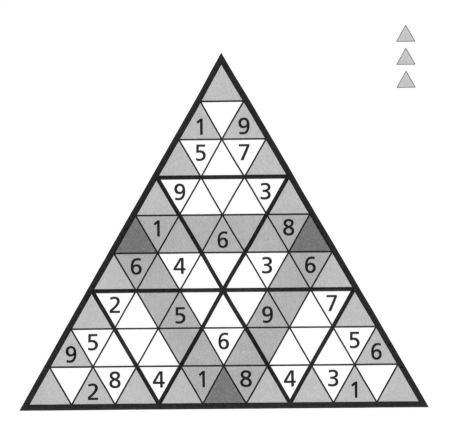

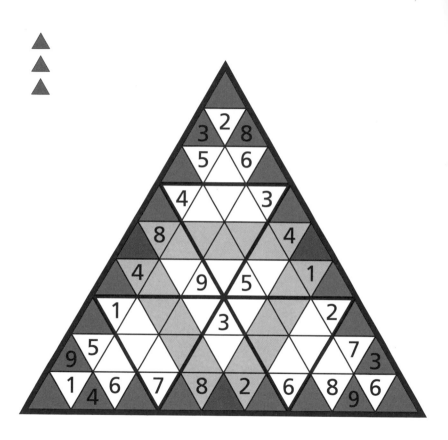

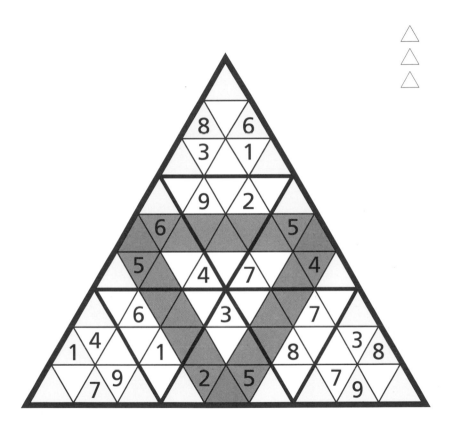

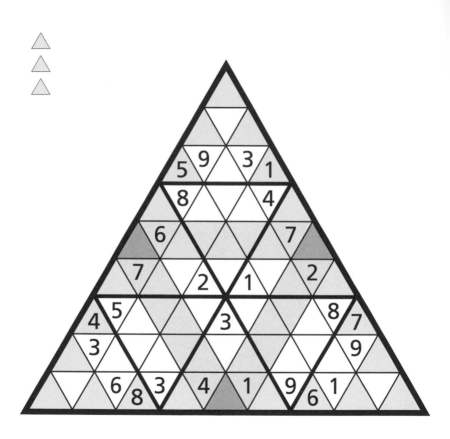

112

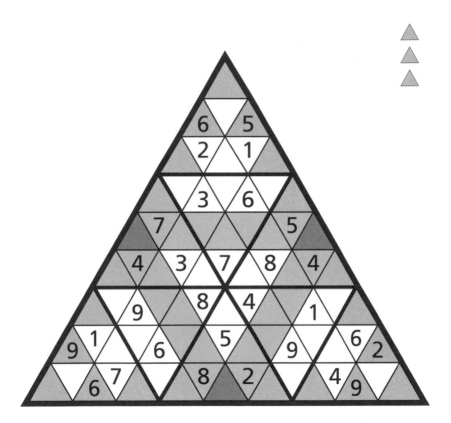

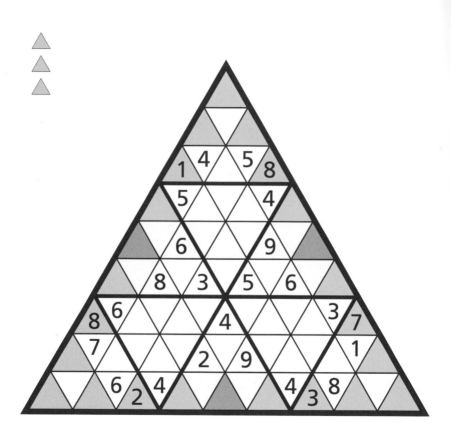

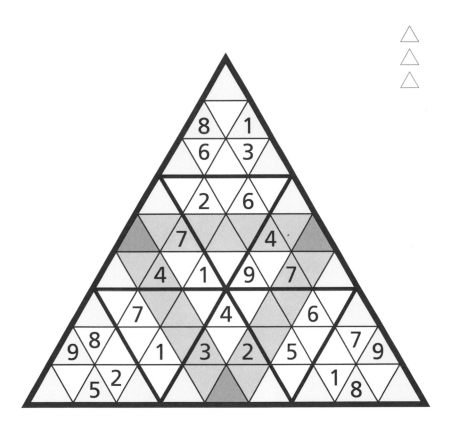

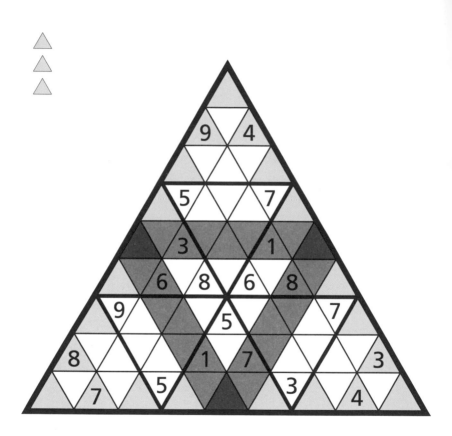

116

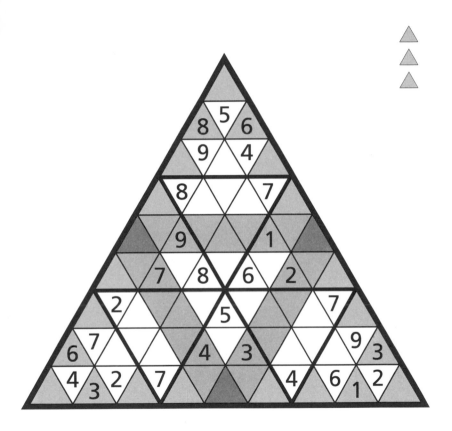

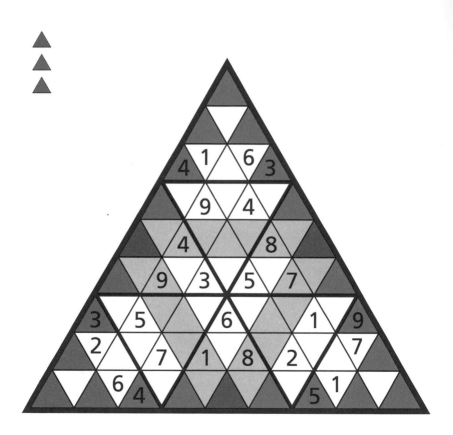

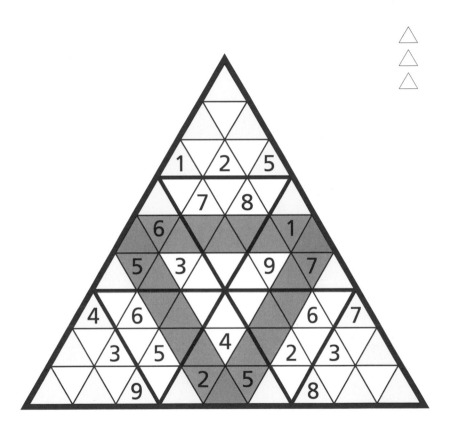

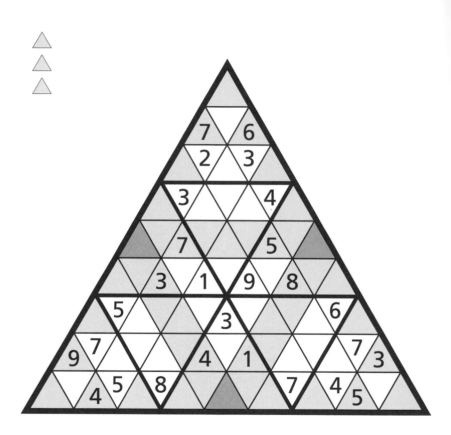

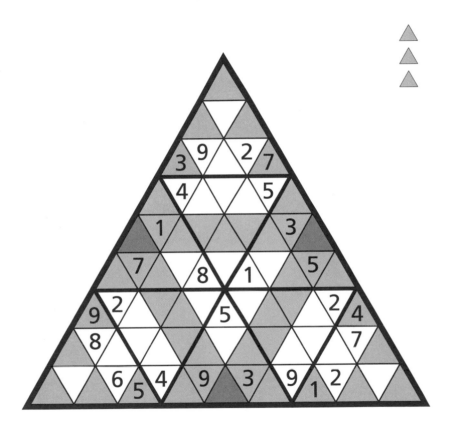

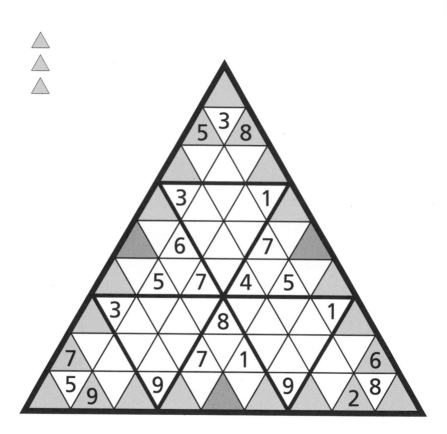

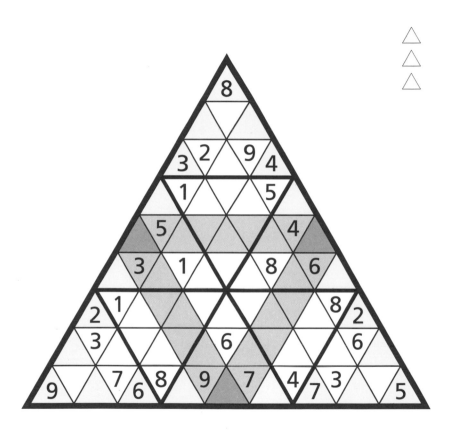

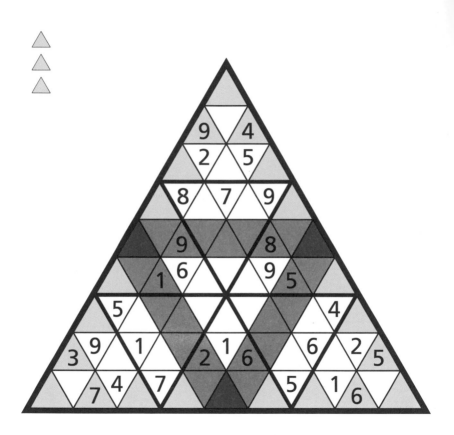

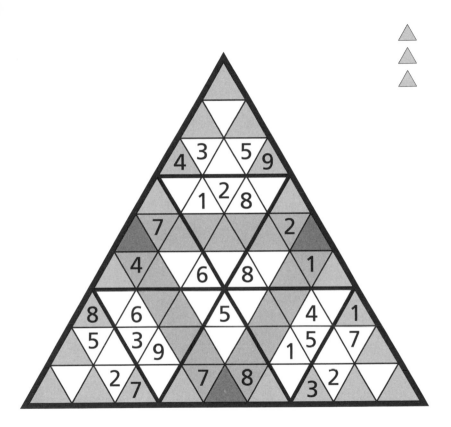

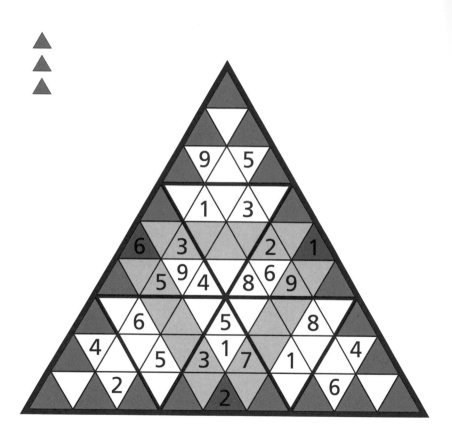

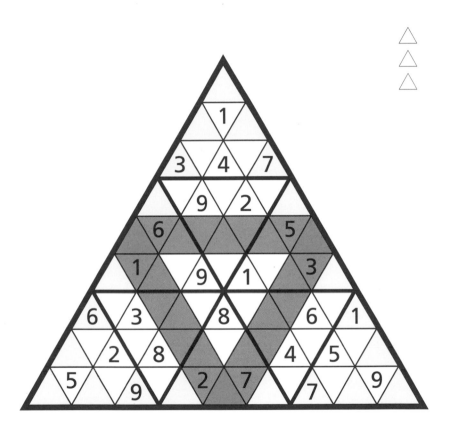

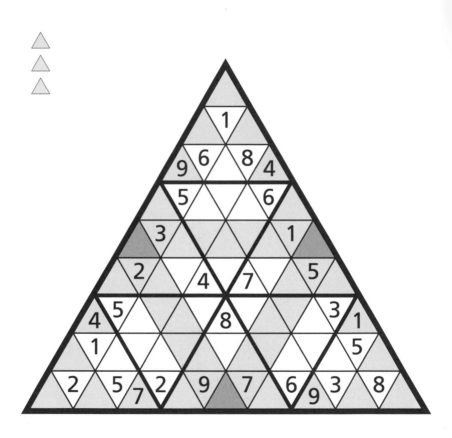

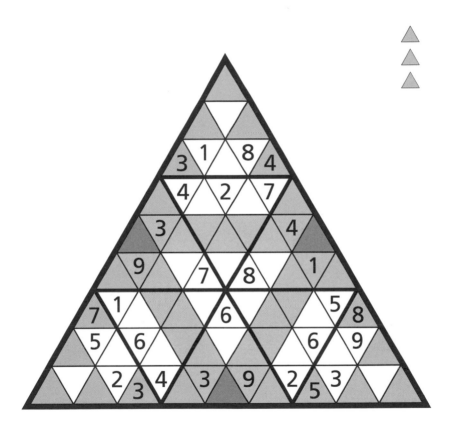

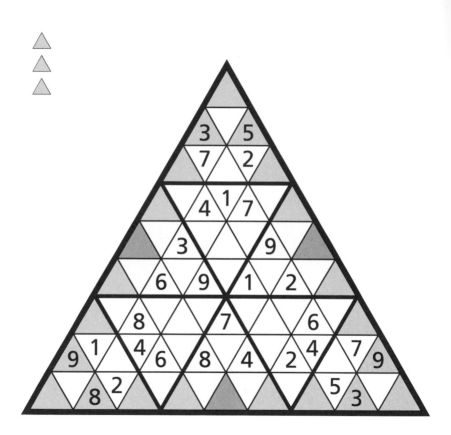

130

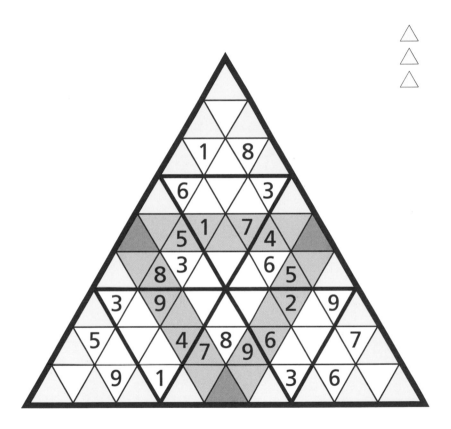

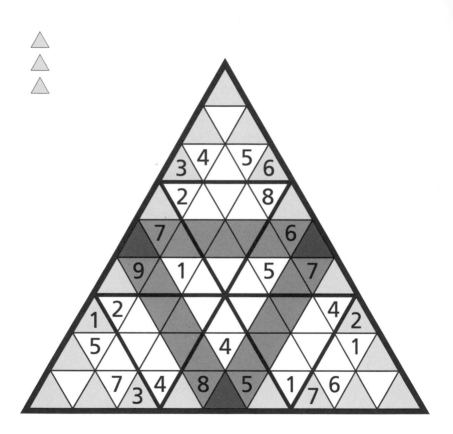

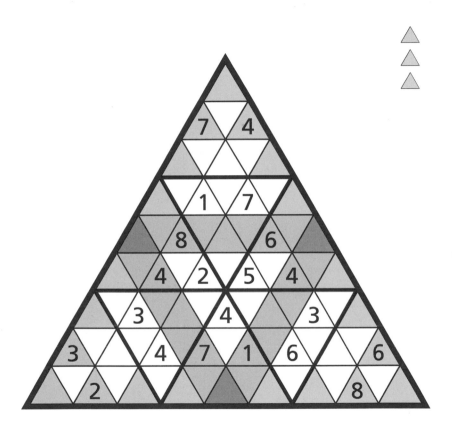

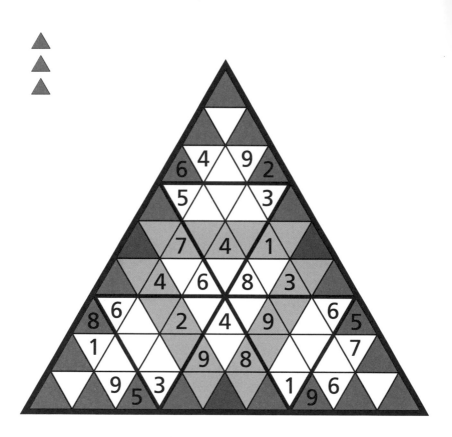

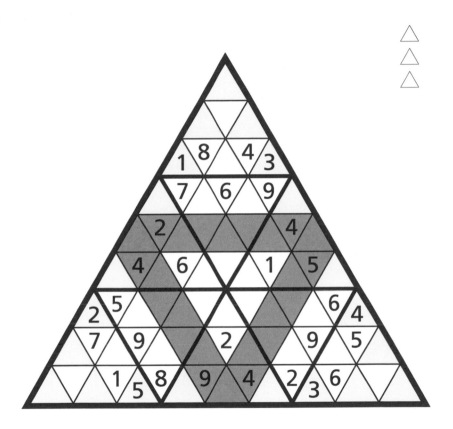

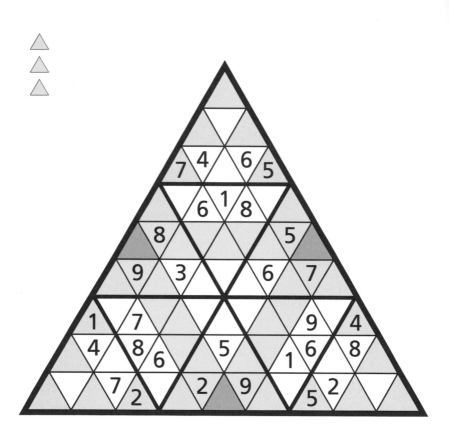

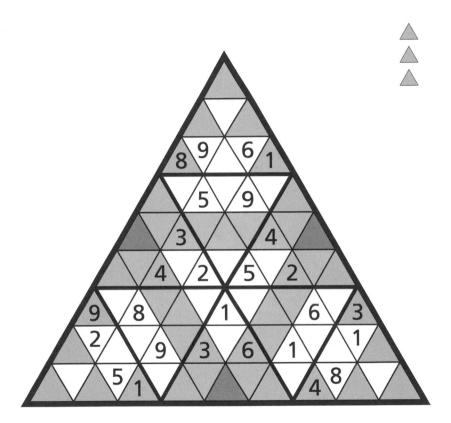

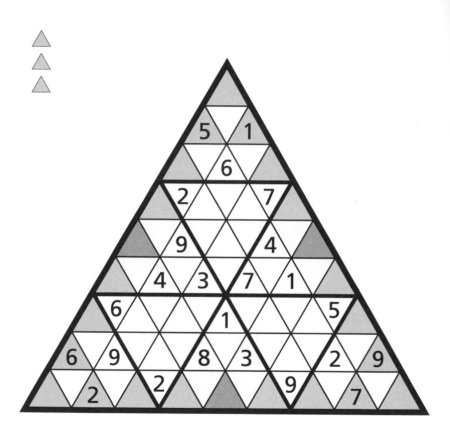

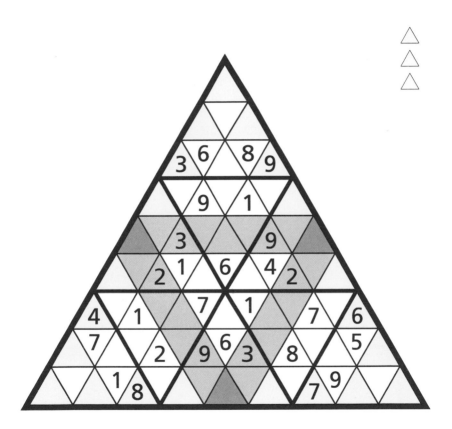

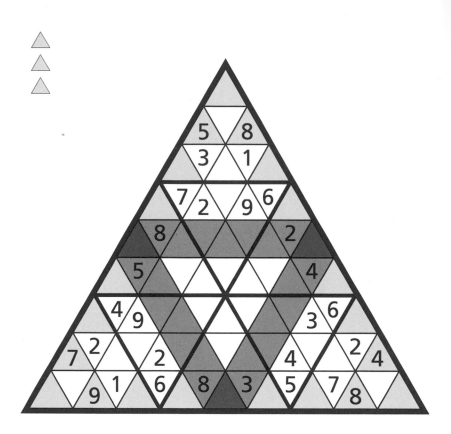

140

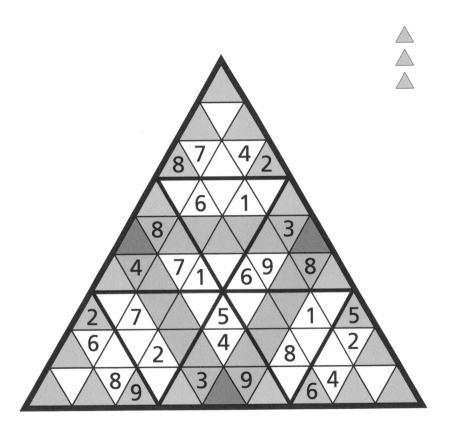

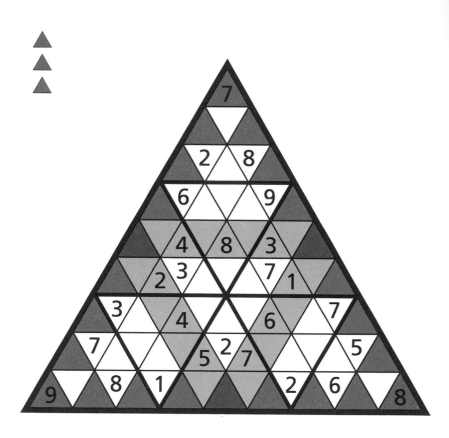

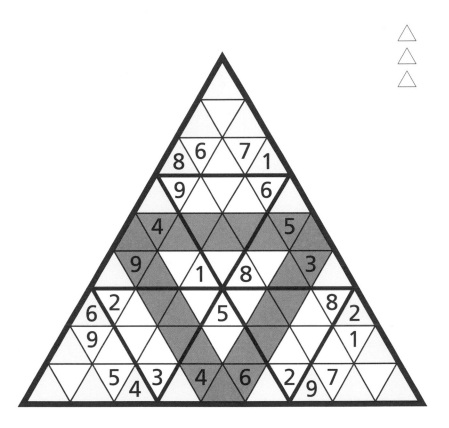

143

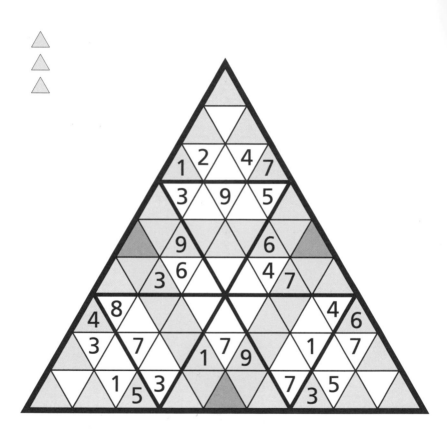

144

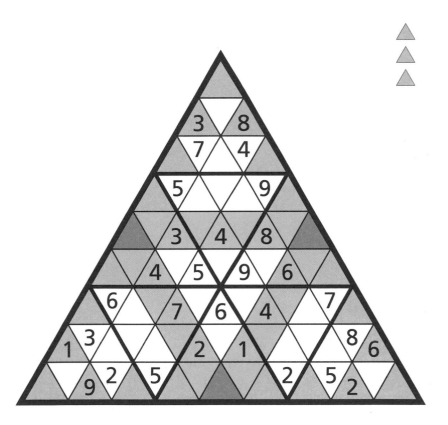

145

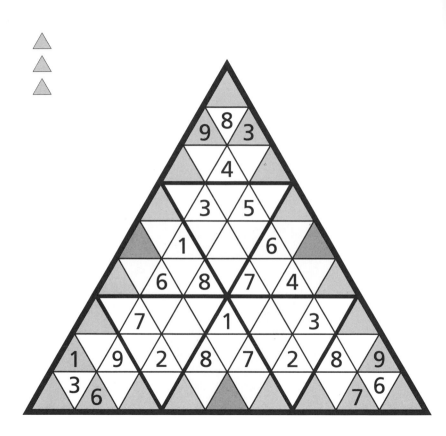

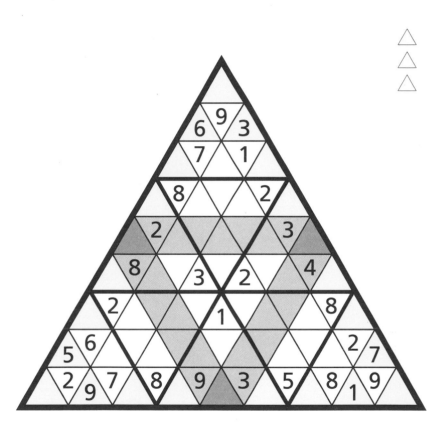

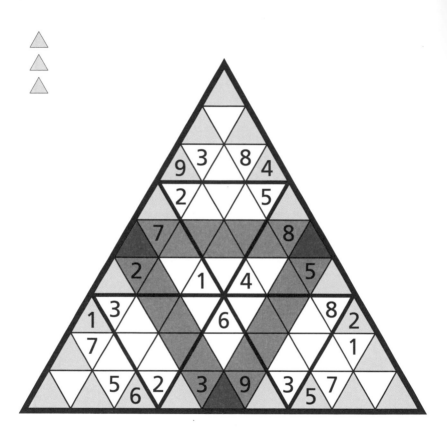

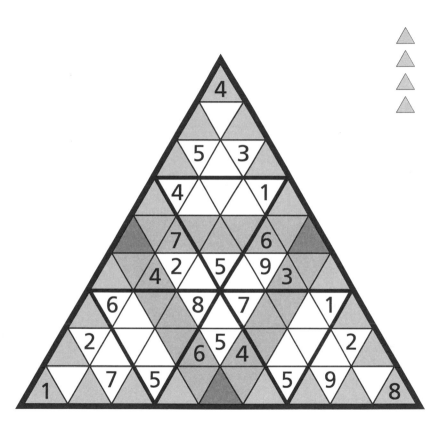

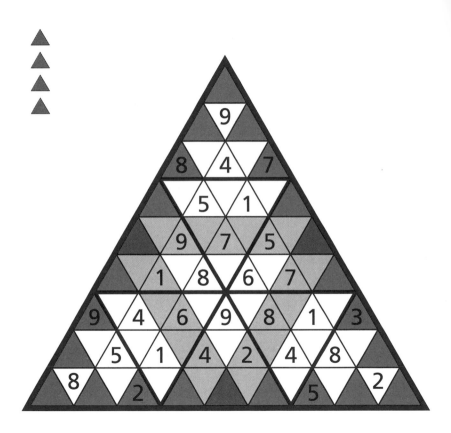

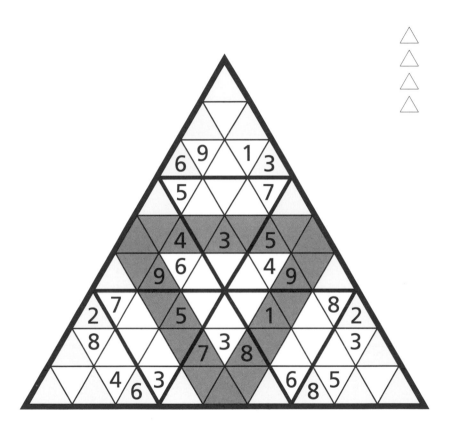

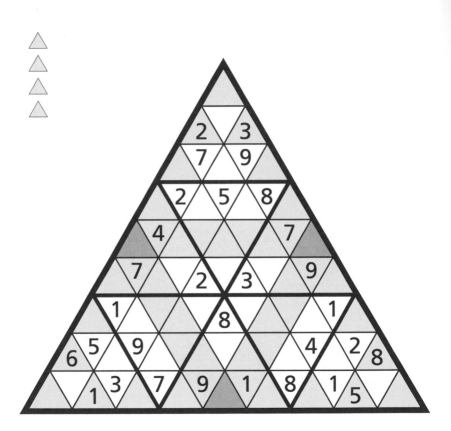

152

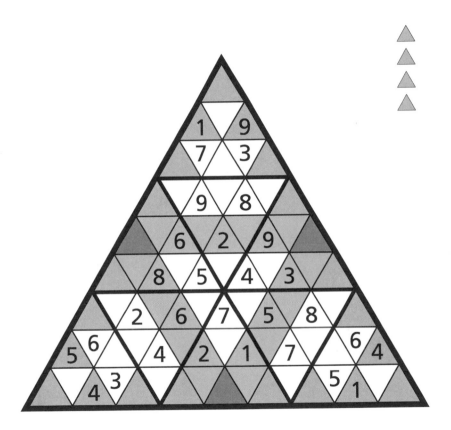

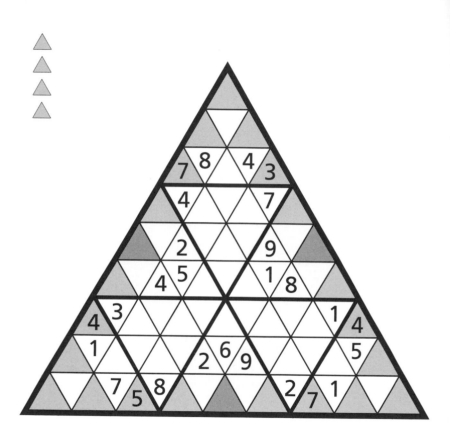

154

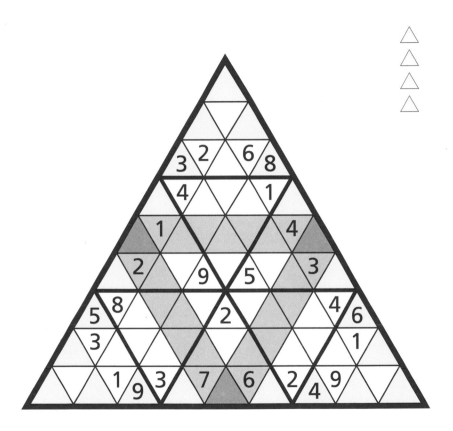

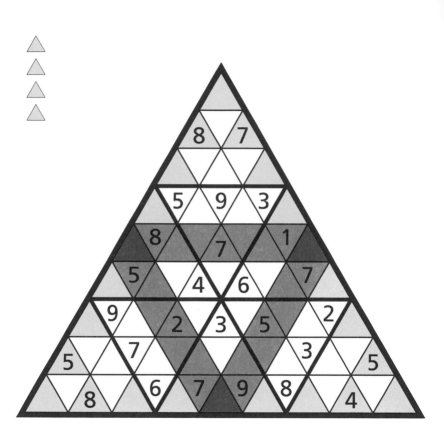

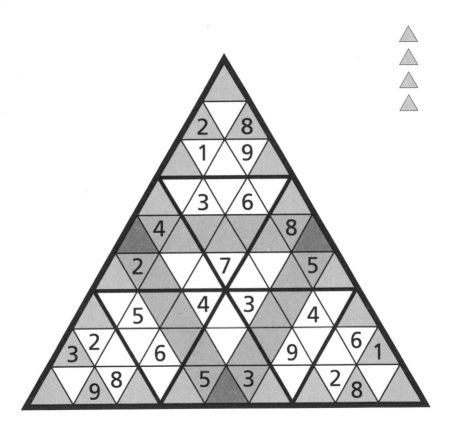

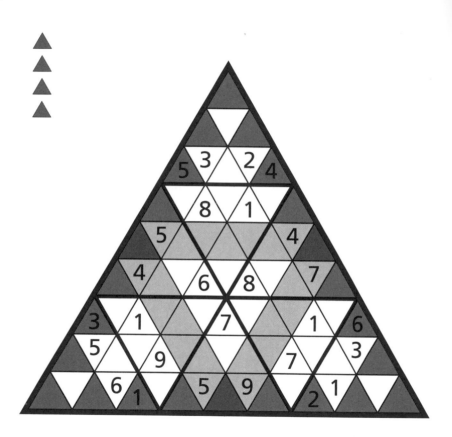

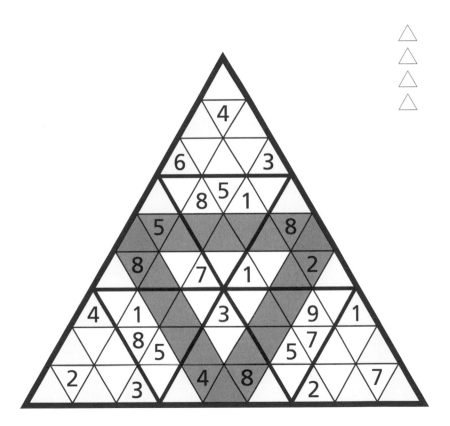

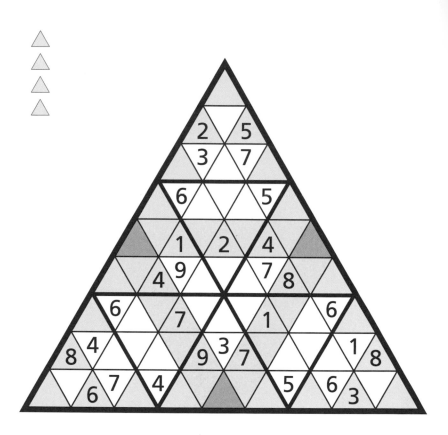

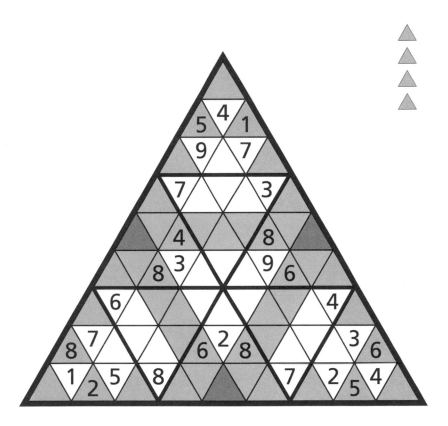

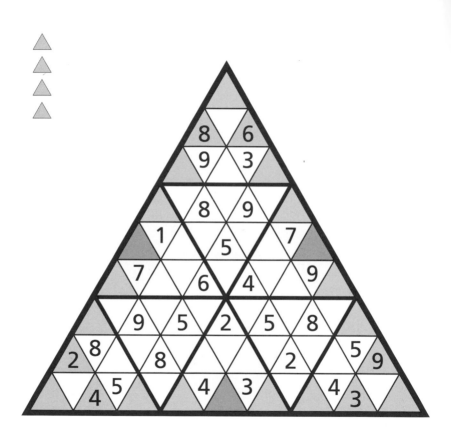

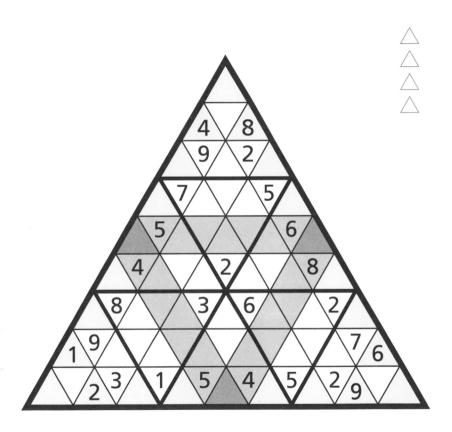

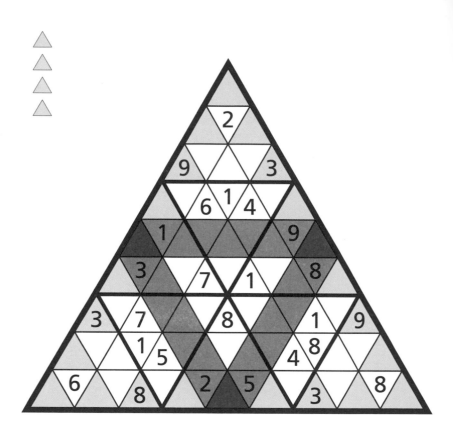

164

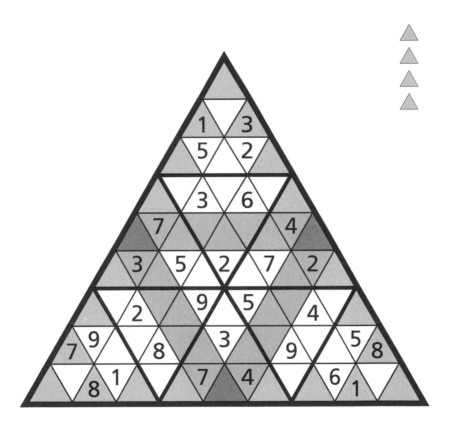

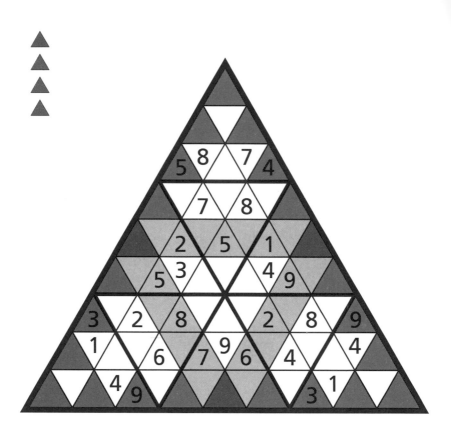

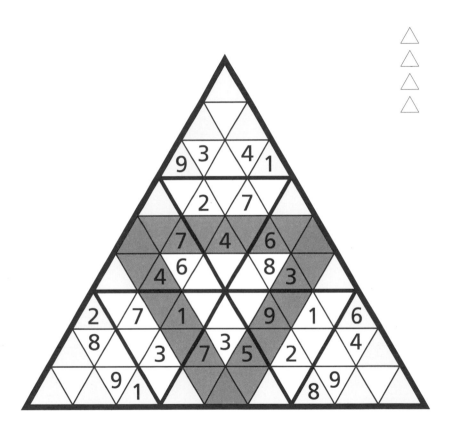

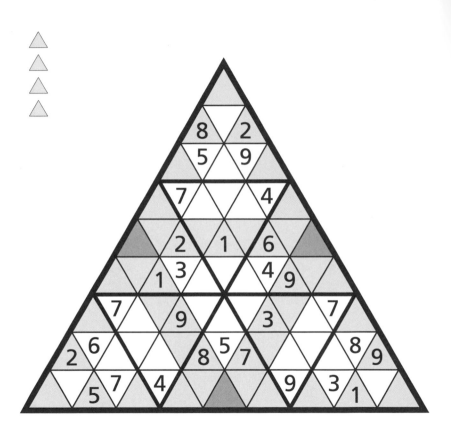

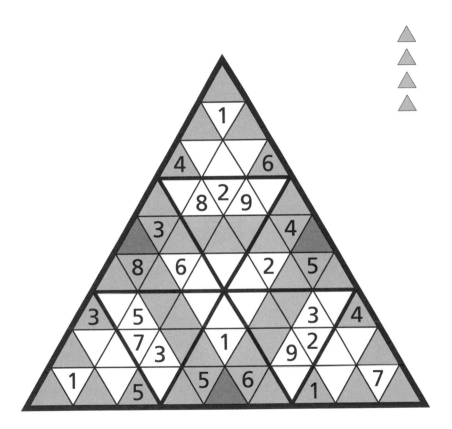

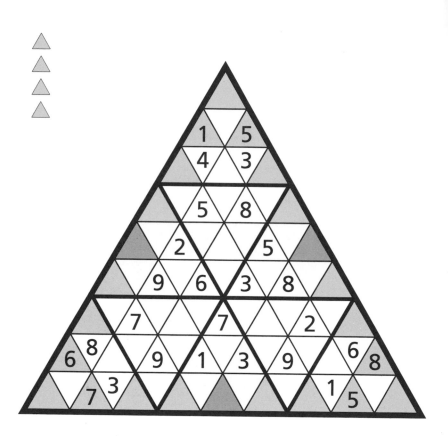

170

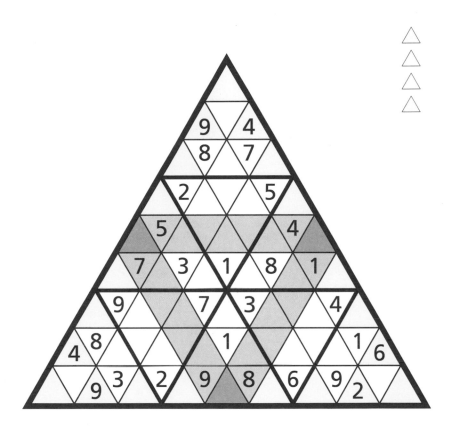

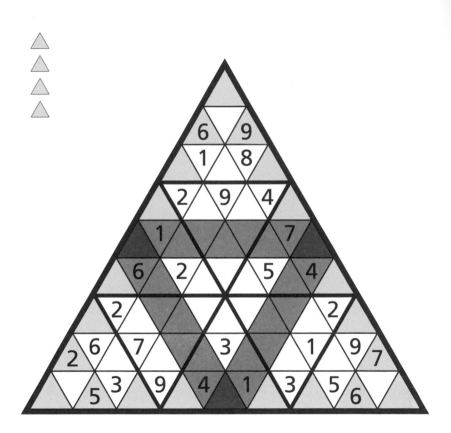

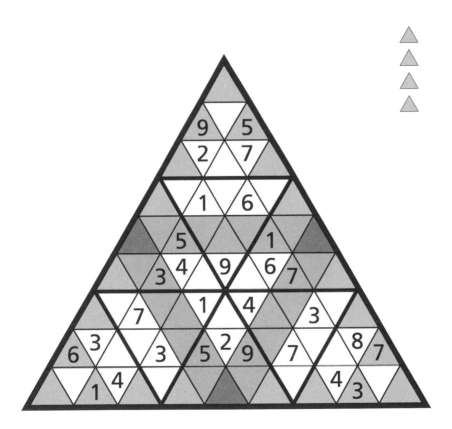

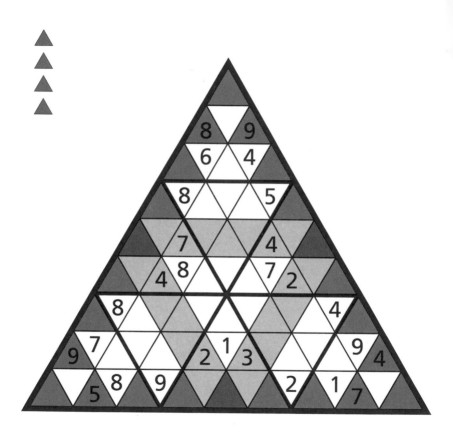

174

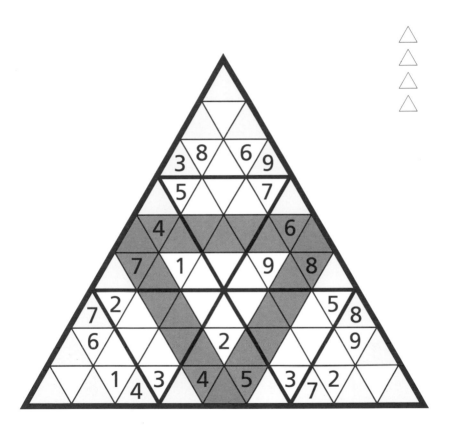

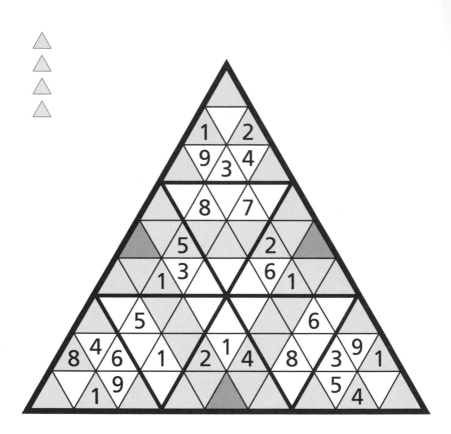

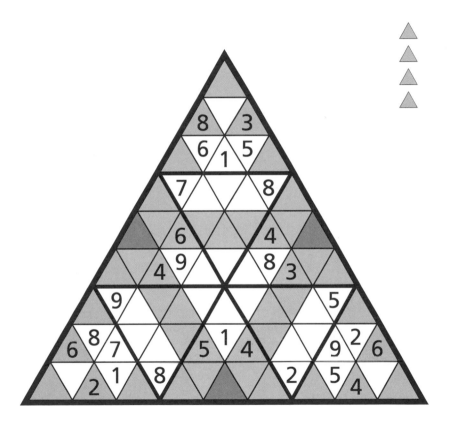

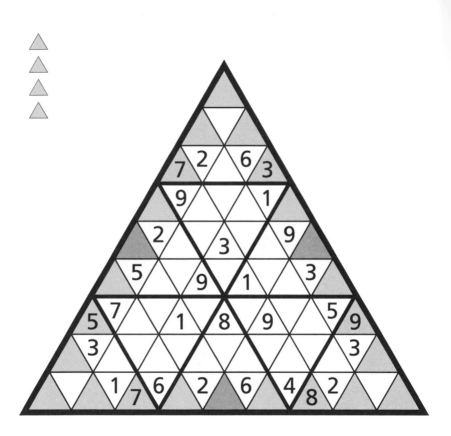

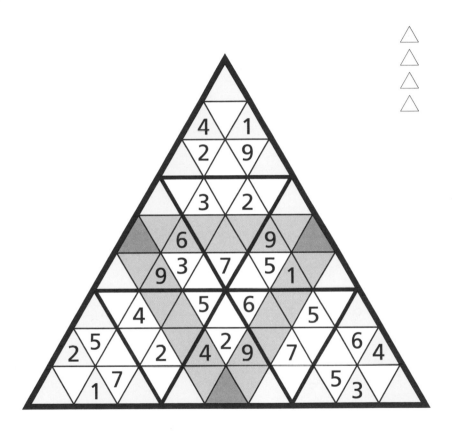

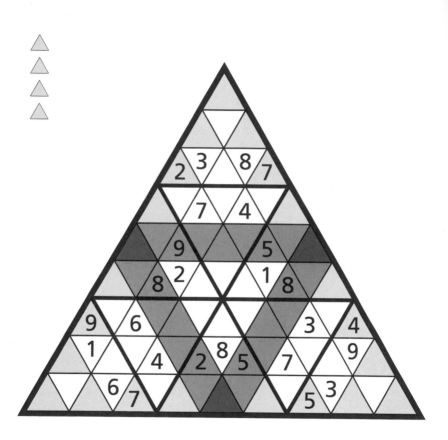

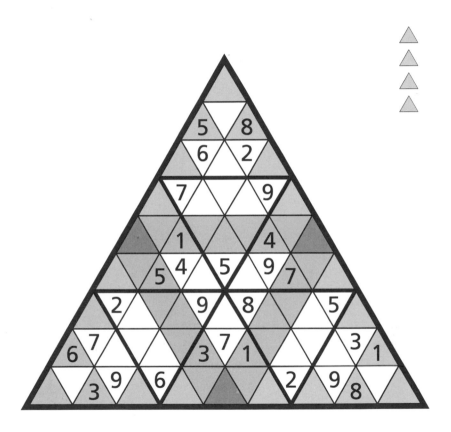

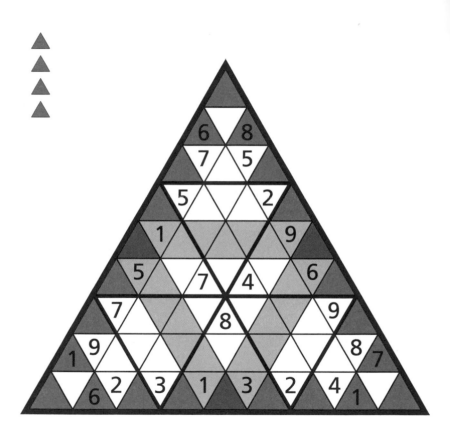

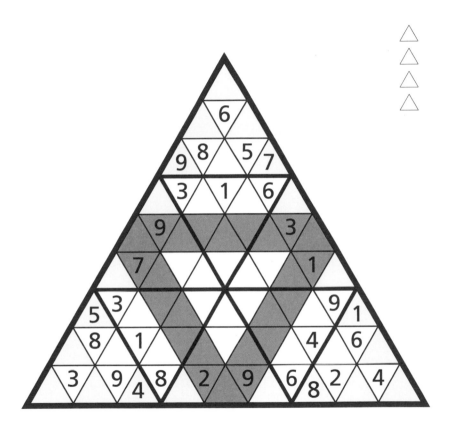

183

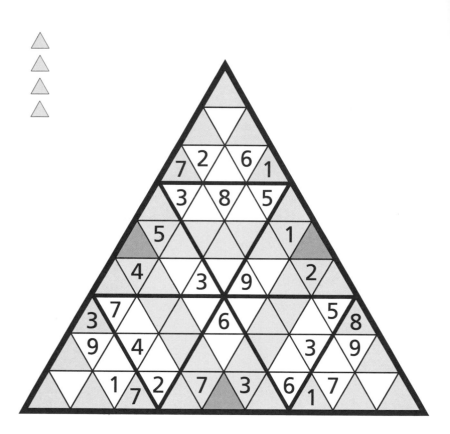

184

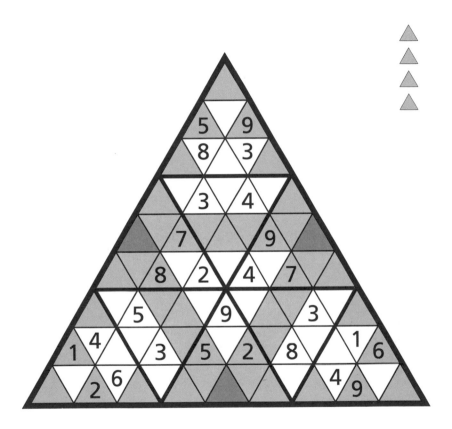

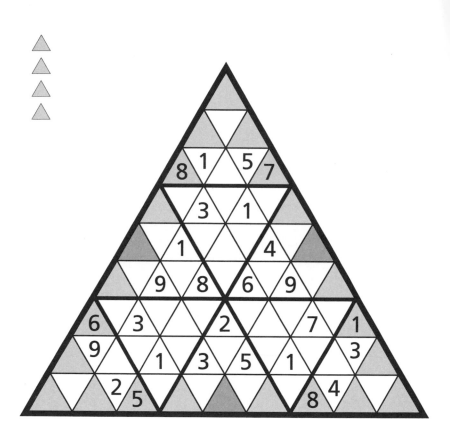

186

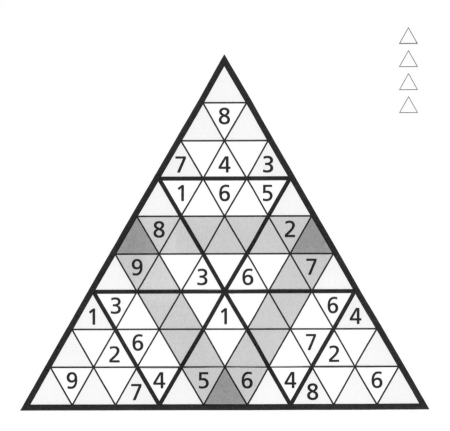

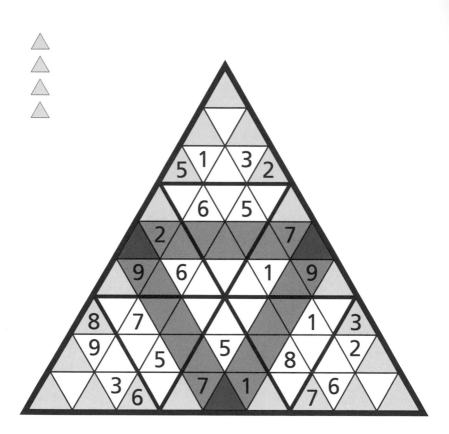

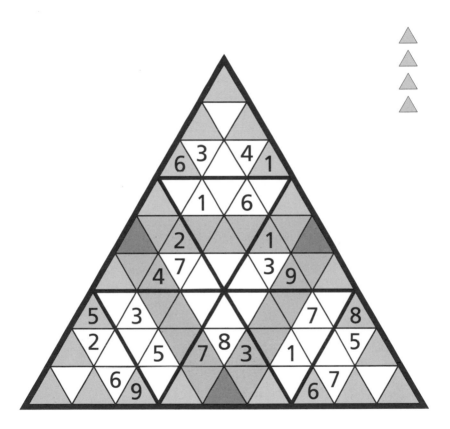

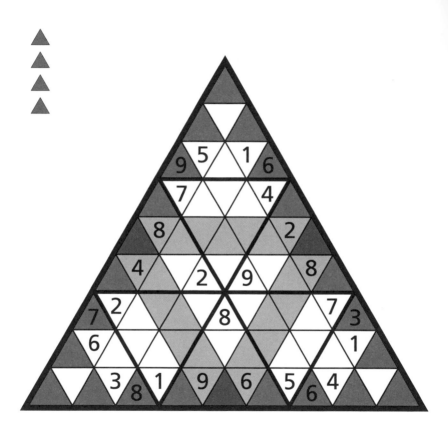

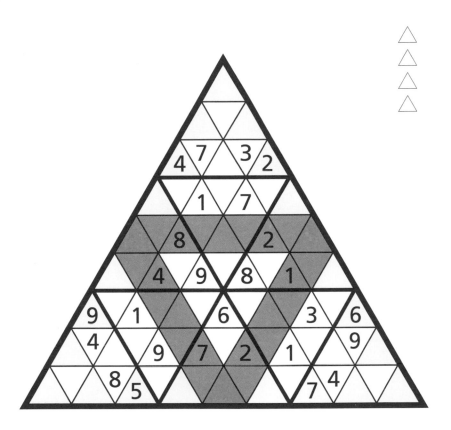

191

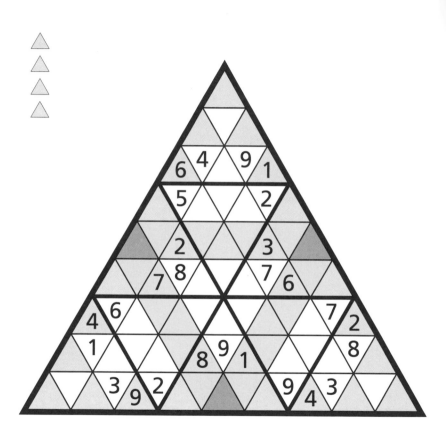

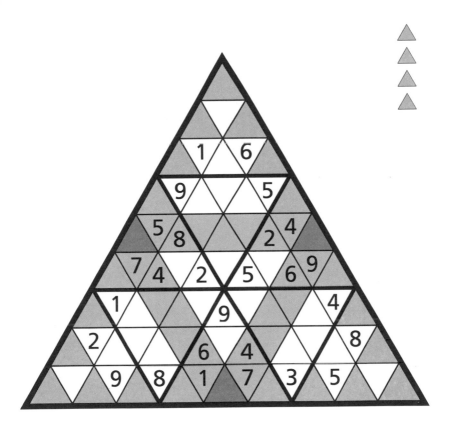

ANSWERS

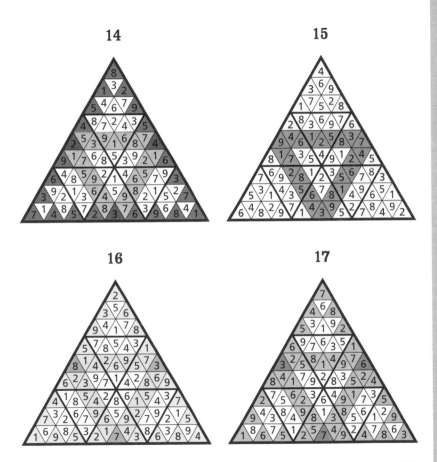

195

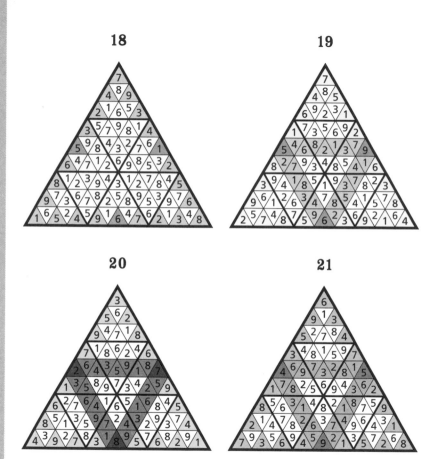

18

19

20

21

196

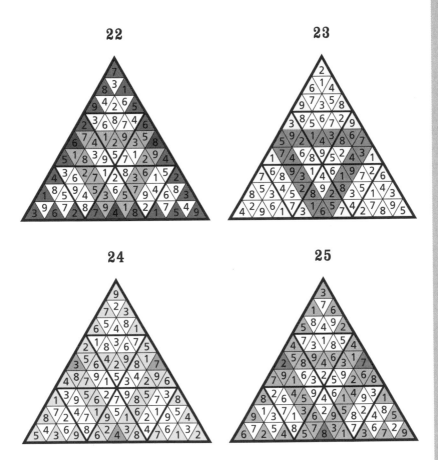

26

27

28

29

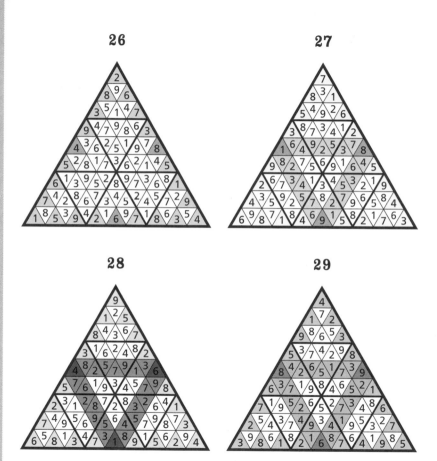

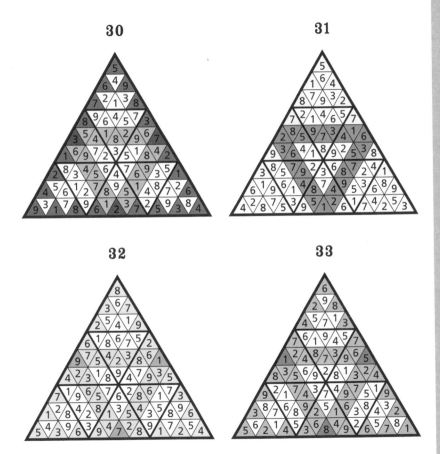

30

31

32

33

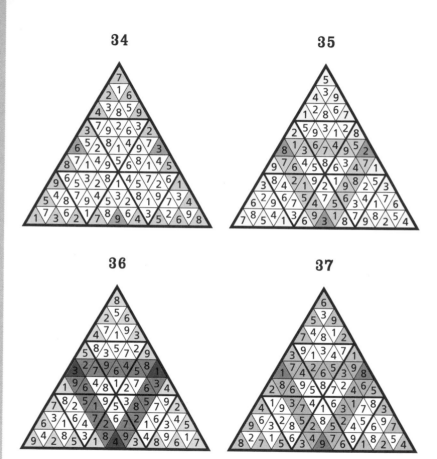

34

35

36

37

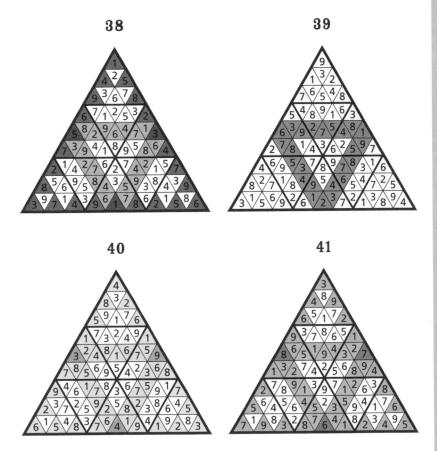

38

39

40

41

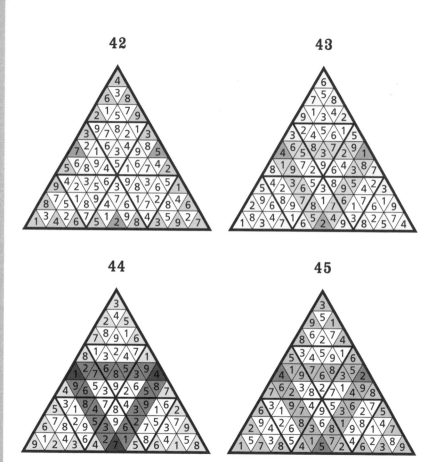

46

47

48

49

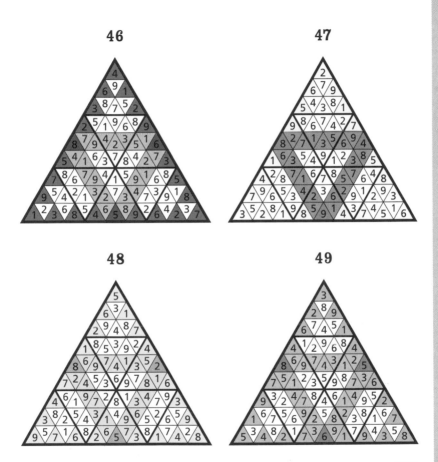

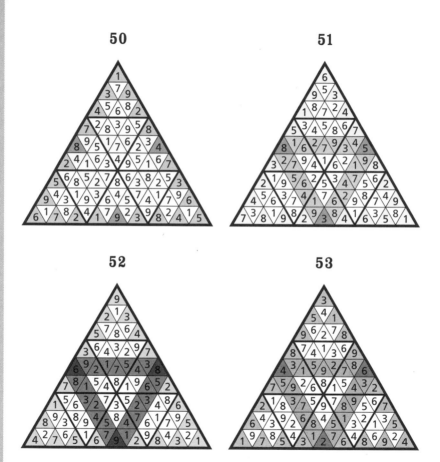

204

54

55

56

57

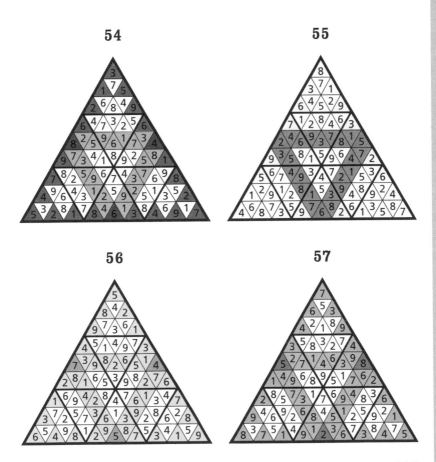

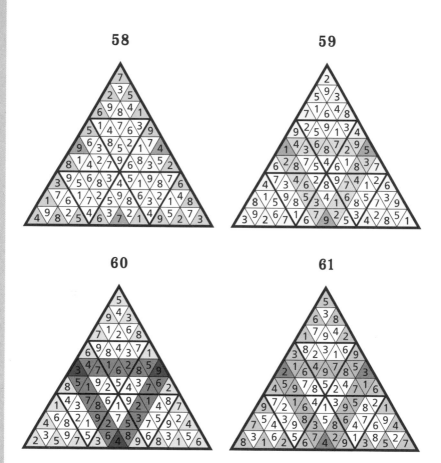

58

59

60

61

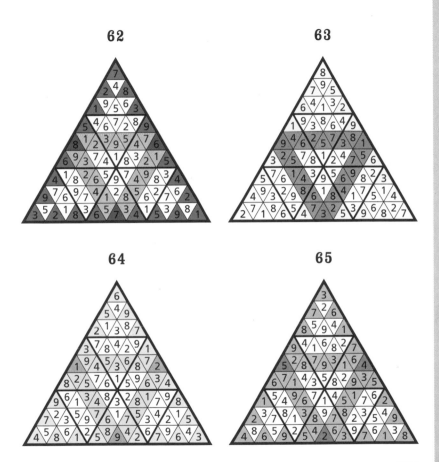

62

63

64

65

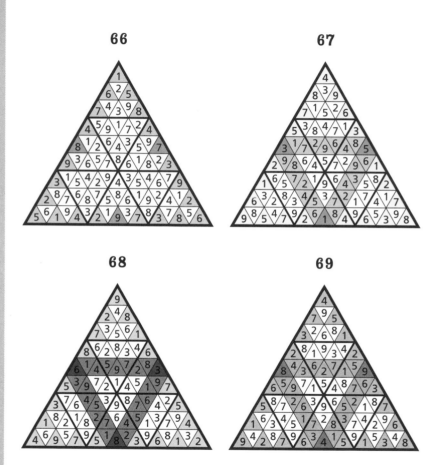

66

67

68

69

208

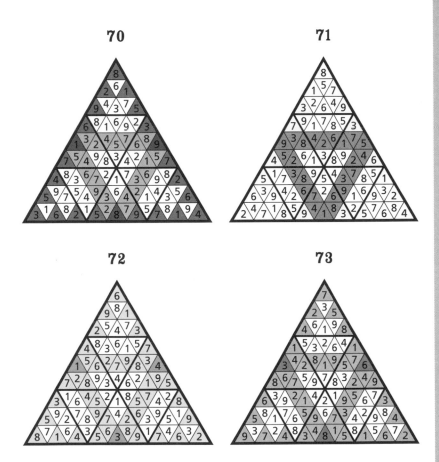

70

71

72

73

209

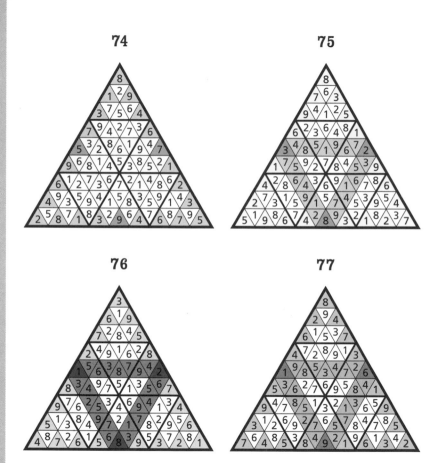

74 75 76 77

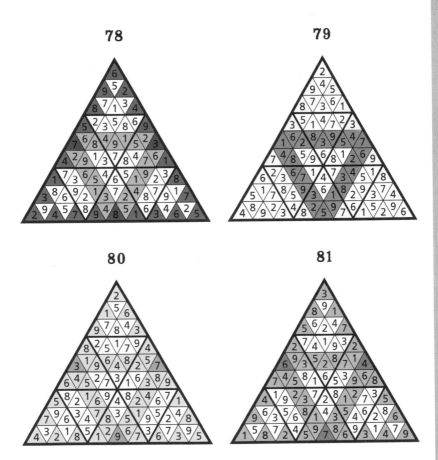

78 79

80 81

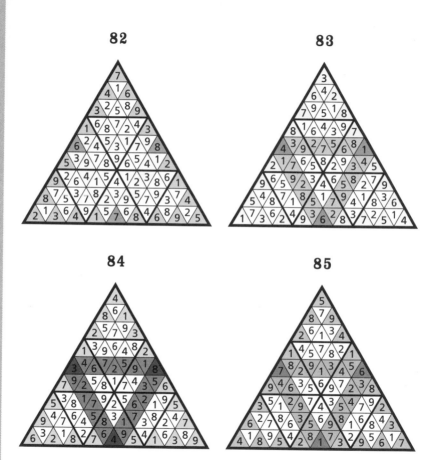

82

83

84

85

212

86

87

88

89

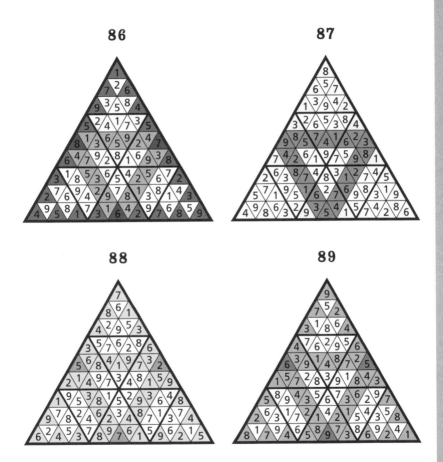

90

91

92

93

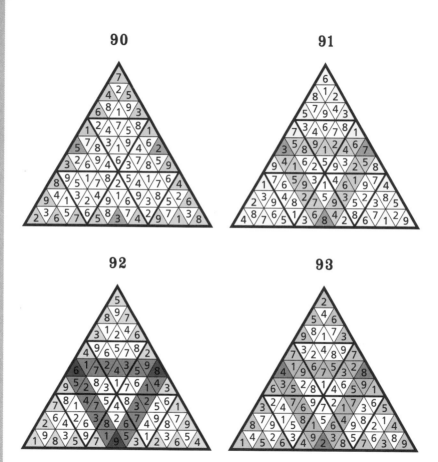

214

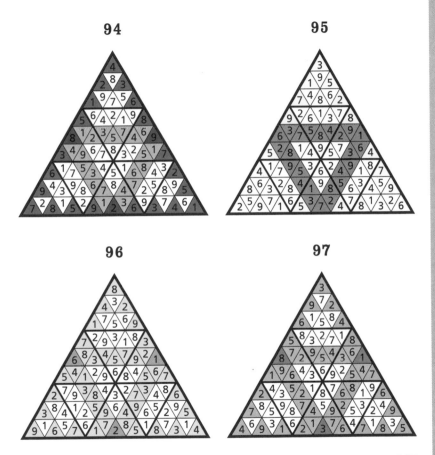

94

95

96

97

98

99

100

101

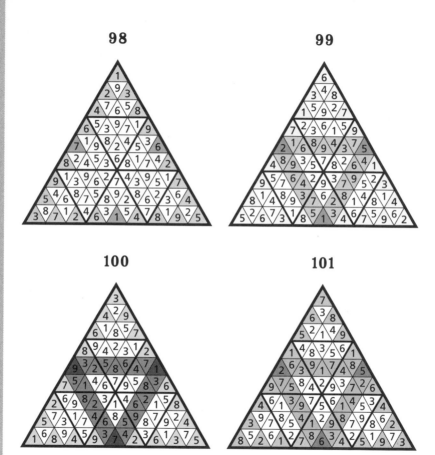

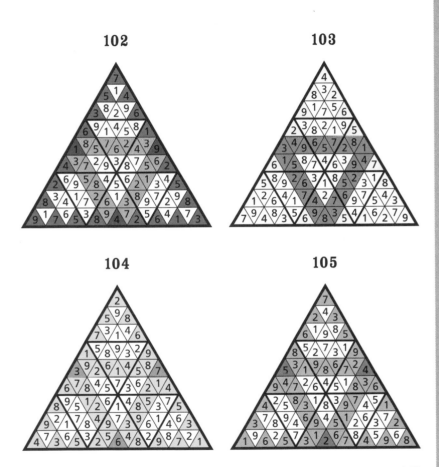

102

103

104

105

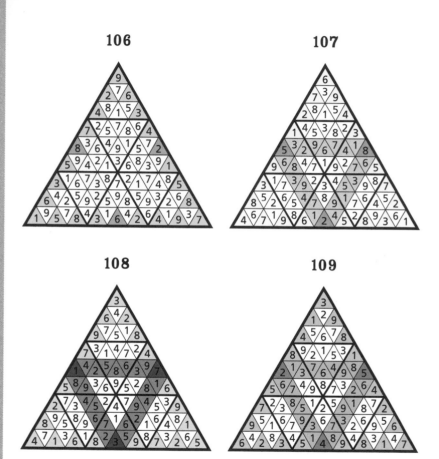

110

111

112

113

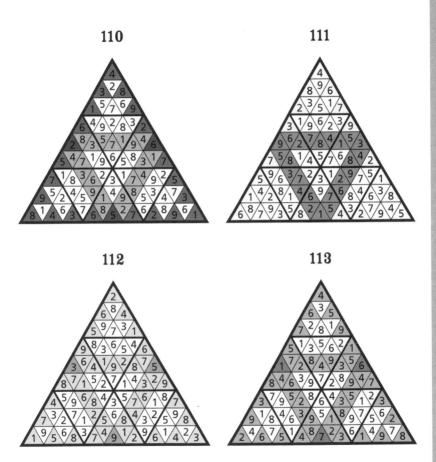

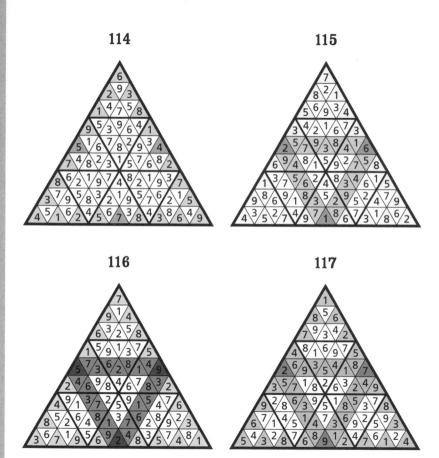

114

115

116

117

118

119

120

121

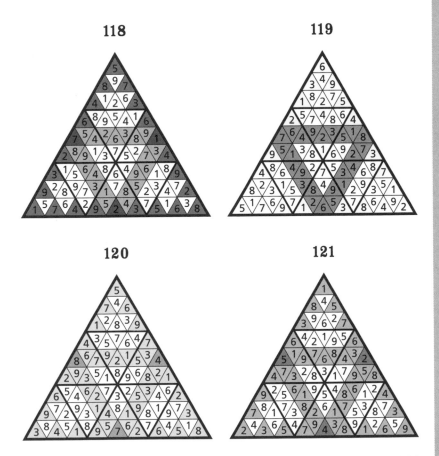

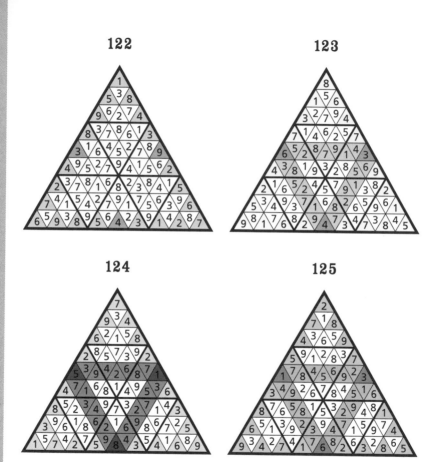

122

123

124

125

126

127

128

129

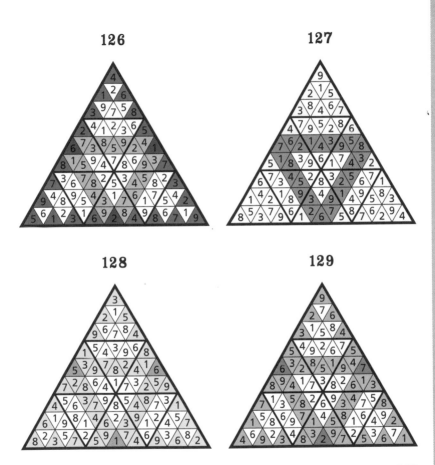

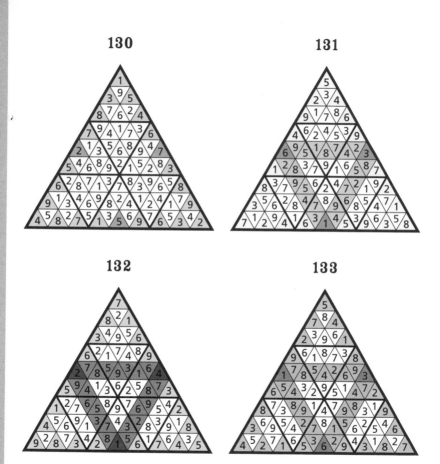

130

131

132

133

224

134

135

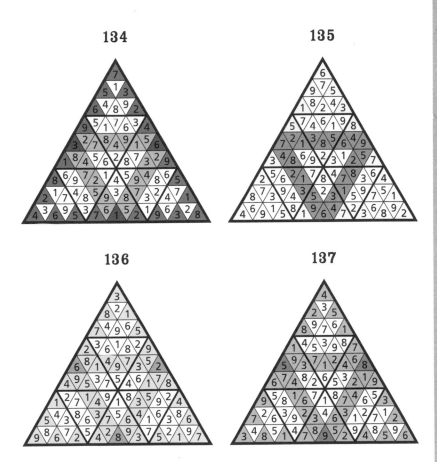

136

137

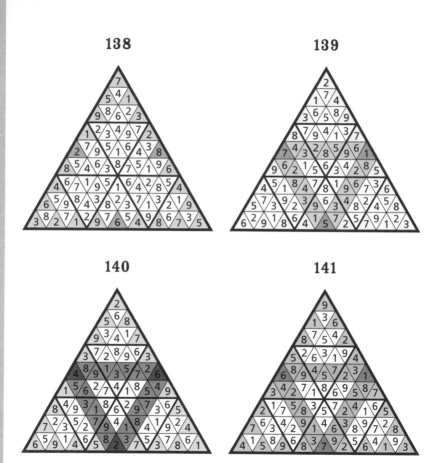

138

139

140

141

142

143

144

145

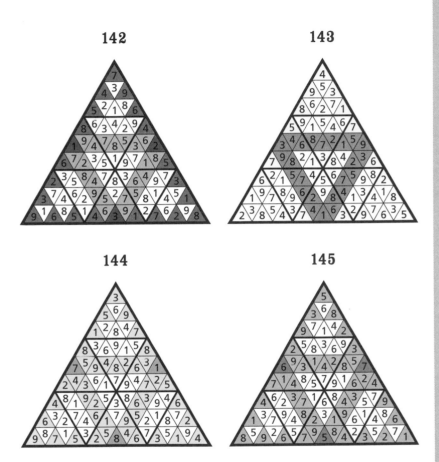

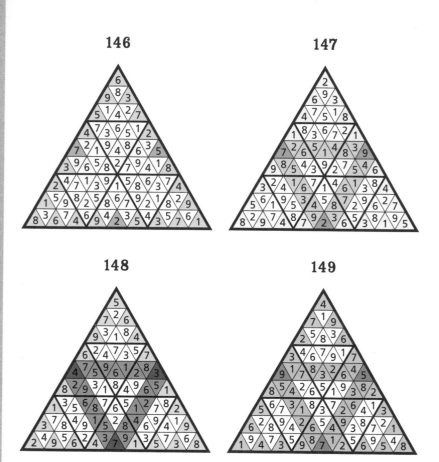

146   147

148   149

228

150

151

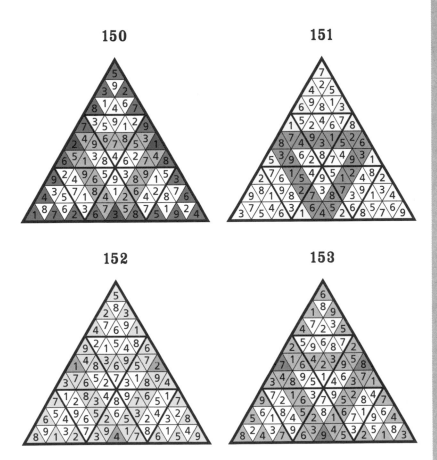

152

153

154

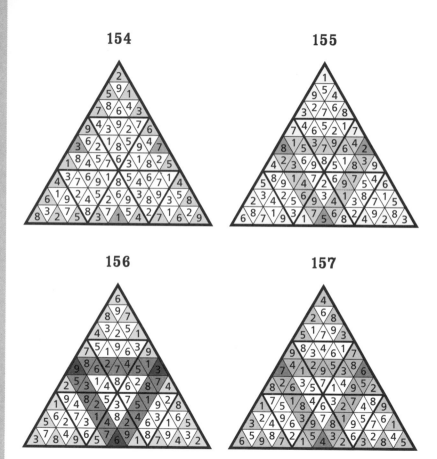

155

156

157

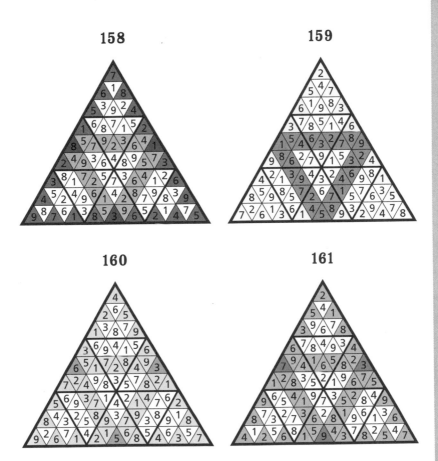

158

159

160

161

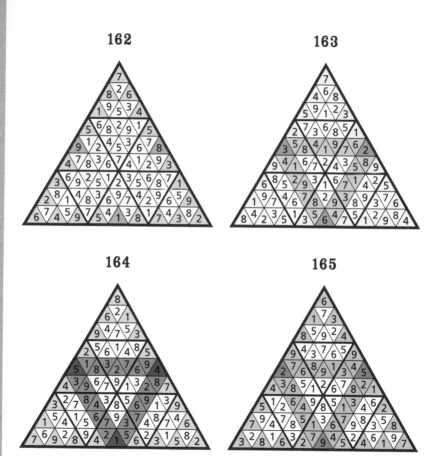

162 163 164 165

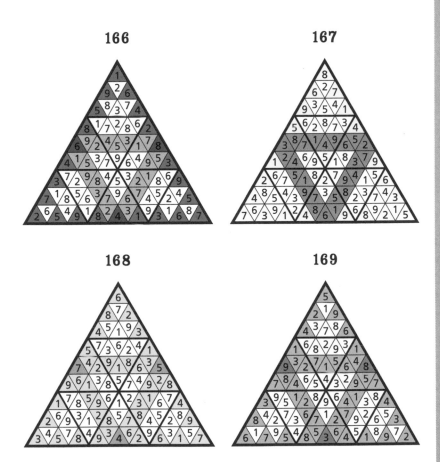

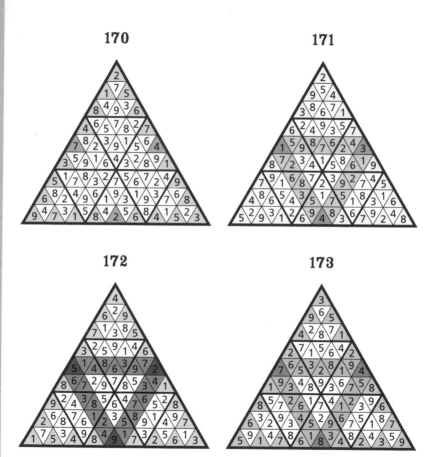

170

171

172

173

234

174

175

176

177

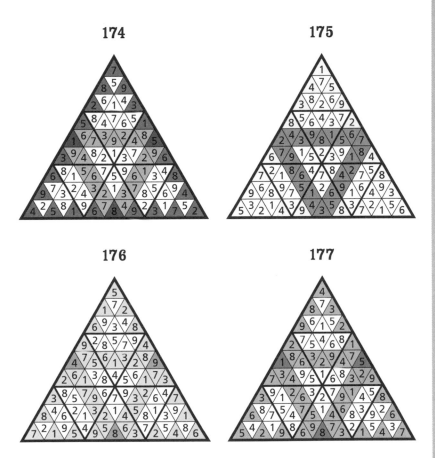

178

179

180

181

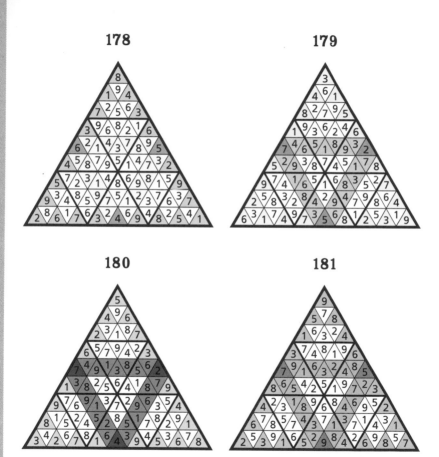

236

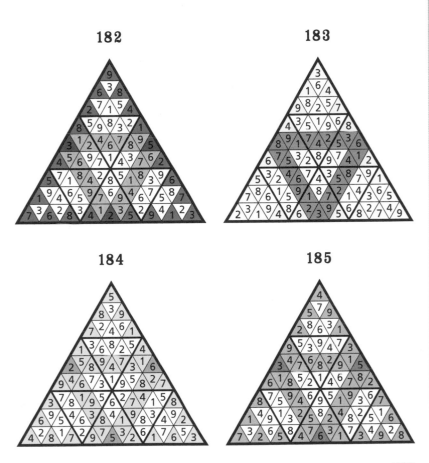

182

183

184

185

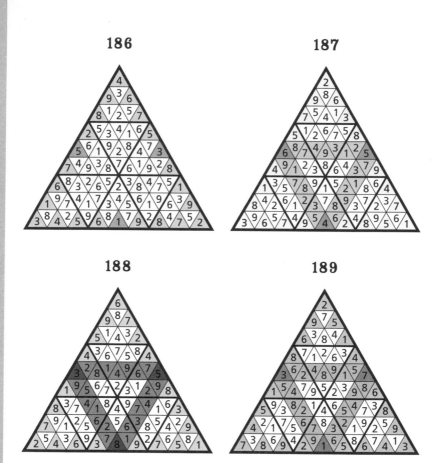

186

187

188

189

238

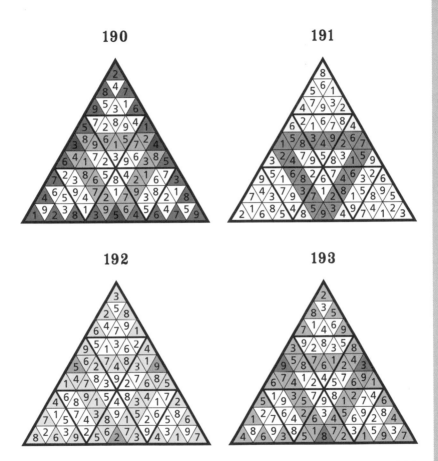

190 191 192 193

ABOUT THE AUTHOR

Japheth J. Light attended Clemson University, where he earned a bachelor's degree and a master's degree in electrical engineering. He also received a master's degree in mathematics from the Florida Institute of Technology. Light lives in Palm Bay, Florida, with his wife, Monica, and their children, Julie and Evan. He currently works as a software engineer and teaches math for Keiser University. In addition to Tridoku, Light has developed Snowflake Sudoku, a hexagonal version of sudoku.